THE
BUZZARD BUTTE POACHERS

Wrestling, Rodeo, and Bad Guys

Shane Woods Series
Book Three

Dr. Tom Latham

DynoTech Publishing

Edited and published by Dave Carlson at DynoTech Publishing, Colorado Springs, Colorado, USA. (www.dynotech.com)

ISBN: 978-1-885708-53-3 (Paperback)

Library of Congress Control Number: 2026904687

First Printing: 2026

Contents

Shane Latham practiced soccer in his Pillsbury Baptist Bible College (PBBC) uniform.

DEDICATION

I dedicate this book to our second son, Shane Thomas Latham, who was born on December 2, 1970. I remember rushing to the hospital through the nose-nipping Minnesota cold. Our family, nestled deep in the frozen tundra of Minneapolis, received the gift of another boy. We were overjoyed to have him.

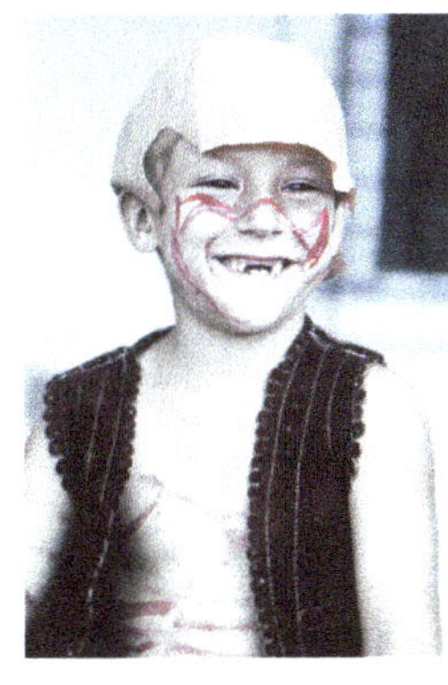

As Shane grew, he quickly became a lively playmate and wrestling partner for his older brother, Thomas. His boundless energy during our roughhousing sessions once left him with a gapped grin when he knocked out his own two front baby teeth.

With TV absent during the first four years of our marriage, both boys learned many Bible verses. Shane, charmingly pronouncing "L" like "Y," made us smile when he said, "I yove da Yord." At age four, after being caught red-handed taking a cookie he was told not to touch, he realized he was a sinner. His mother, Penny, gently guided him to understand forgiveness and salvation. Shane humbly prayed to Jesus to save him.

As the years passed and Shane entered adolescence, he exhibited his energetic nature in everything he did—often twirling his arms and jumping from one thing to another. Running and spinning down the hallway caused Penny to affectionately call him "Twirley Jerk." His daring spirit led to more emergency room trips than Thomas and Kosy combined.

This drive extended into Shane's academic life. He skipped a year in his Accelerated Christian Education Paces to graduate high school alongside Thomas, allowing them both to start Pillsbury Baptist Bible College together. There, Shane joined the soccer and wrestling teams.

We were excited for Shane when he married Erin Lynch from Belgrade, Montana. During our furlough, they filled our roles in Brazil. Penny and I loved being nearby as they raised Camila and Gabriel.

Our professional relationship deepened over 20 years in the wrestling ministry, where our collaboration took on greater meaning as we saw many come to know Christ through this effective and enjoyable sport.

Today, Shane is a wonderful husband, dad, and grandfather. I'm grateful to see his children and my great-grandchildren weekly—a surprising blessing. Now, the Latham family even includes third-generation missionaries, furthering our legacy.

Currently, Shane leads a home cell group upstairs, focusing on spiritual growth. His Jiu-Jitsu state champion belt prominently adorns the wall.

Beyond our family bond, I consider Shane a mentor and counselor—a rare and treasured part of our father-son relationship. Looking ahead, I find comfort knowing that, as I live out my years with Shane and Erin upstairs, they'll care for me when the time comes.

INTRODUCTION

Storytelling is one of my passions, and through my books, I strive to convey joy, encourage reflection on my faith, and move readers emotionally by sharing real-life experiences. If my stories move you emotionally, I have succeeded.

I am committed to presenting Christ as the only true Savior, and to showing that following Him wholeheartedly defines authentic Christian living. I also reveal the devastating impact the liquor industry had on my family, hoping to illustrate the destruction it can cause. It's a legal drug that sent my mother to prison and caused the death of my brother, Danny, at 49 years old.

Abandoned three times by my mother, I found refuge with my loving grandparents at their Crabtree Creek farm. Their care shaped my life. I have no idea where I would be today if it weren't for the tender care of my grandfather, John Taylor, and his wonderful wife, Julia. Certainly, I wouldn't be where I am.

This book is written to inspire you to accept Christ as your Savior and commit fully to Him. My own journey began on May 6, 1964, when a fellow sailor, Richard Edwards, invited me to Calvary Baptist Church in San Francisco, California. During my Navy service, Richard and I shared our faith with others during sea voyages.

I spent ten years in formal Bible study. Our family arrived in Brazil on October 1, 1976. We started four churches, and I now pastor the fourth.

Some images and illustrations in this book were generated or enhanced using artificial intelligence (AI) technology to enrich your experience as a reader.

Dr. Tom Latham
Missionary and Wrestling Coach in Brazil

1 - Hiding From Vini the Fin

Loretta Woods—now calling herself Linda Olson—was hiding from evil men seeking the $10,000 she owed them. Her addiction and lack of a poker face had left her in the lurch, ruining her life and that of her three children.

She regretted leaving her three children but reasoned, "They'll be better off at Grandpa's farm in Oregon. He'll take care of them like before."

Working at The Crab Shack on Fisherman's Wharf was the best way to lay low. Who would look for her among Bay Area seafood? She hoped no one would.

She lived above the restaurant because Dwayne Spear saw she needed help and he needed a waitress. She figured no one would look for her here. WRONG!

She had just started her shift, adjusting her apron and checking her order book, when Vini the Fin entered with his crew. She panicked, scrambling for a strategy as her heart raced and may have skipped a few beats.

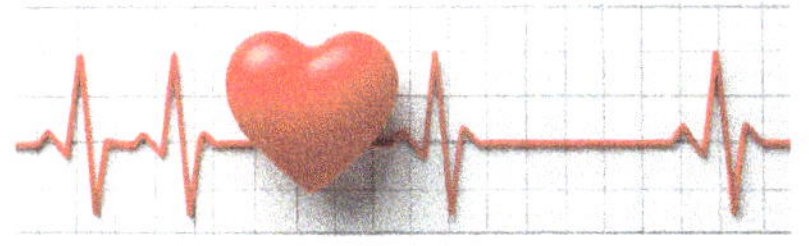

Changing her name to Linda Olson would not be enough to fool Vini. She needed to disappear quickly. Rocky, the man who cleared the tables, noticed the fear in her face and quickly came to her side, "Linda, what in the world did you see, a ghost?"

She stammered, "I ... I can't talk now. Need to go to my room. Cover for me, okay?"

Rocky was a professional wrestler and no man to fool with. He had a massive physique, bordering on Hulk-like. He would not turn green, but he could make anyone else turn green just by looking askance at them.

Rocky noticed Linda's fear and guessed someone in the restaurant was responsible. He scanned the room for anything odd, found nothing, shrugged, and took Linda's order book to the sharply dressed dudes who had just taken a round table in the far corner of the room.

Vini chatted with his cohorts. "I always keep my back to the wall—like Wild Bill Hickok. No one's shooting me in the back."

Shorty jumped in, "Smart, Boss. Good thing you do—here comes the waiter looking like Boom-Boom Maulhick. Dis dude's a walking fridge."

Rocky took their order—lobster, oysters, scallops, clams, and triple sourdough bread. They were hungry, and the boss was paying. Rocky noticed some tried

 to hide handguns in their shoulder holsters.

He found it odd; the Wharf rarely attracted these types. "You guys are new here, right? I've never seen you before," he said, making conversation as he headed to the kitchen.

Vini sneered, "So, Hulk, you writing a book or moonlighting as a detective? Just get our order, and don't stain your new mommy's apron." His sidekicks snickered, oblivious to the trouble they were asking for.

The big waiter already disliked these men. Their remarks confirmed his impression. Only close friends could call him HULK—not these outsiders. Owner Dwayne Spear witnessed the whole ordeal.

Dwayne couldn't believe the strangers' rudeness and recklessness. He turned to Roberta, the other wairess, "Those guys are dumber than dirt. They just insulted the Bay Area's champion pro wrestler. Maybe we should call back-up." Dwayne was serious, not joking.

Short T. Forsur, truly impressed by Rocky's size, still believed 'the bigger they are, the harder they fall.' But he admitted he couldn't 'fall' someone like Rocky, not in a month of Sundays.

Loretta, once sure Vini had left, sought out Rocky. "Thanks, friend. Migraine hit like a Mack truck. I owe you." She was good at lying and hiding her feelings with a fake smile.

He looked her in the eyes, placing his large hands on her shoulders. "You don't owe me anything." Rocky knew she was lying, but let it go for now. He noticed her frequent nervousness and sometimes smelled liquor on her breath. He would address it later—he never forgot such things.

Rocky Mountain, as he was known in professional wrestling, was no fool. He spent evenings training with massive wrestlers who made bodybuilders look tiny.

He leaned toward Linda. "You know, I used to fool people for a living," he said. "It was pro wrestling, but it was all an act. I can spot when someone's faking it. Let me help you like I helped myself. Maybe we can go to an AA meeting? That's when I took my first steps toward getting better. But honestly, Linda, what you really need is to come to church with me, meet the Great Counselor. He can turn things around for you—and give you eternal life."

He planned to talk to his pastor, Tim Rasmusson, who led him to Jesus and saved his life and marriage. Rocky knew Linda needed this and was determined to help.

After her late-night shift, Loretta staggered to her room and downed several beers before noticing a Gideon Bible in her nightstand drawer. She hadn't seen it before. Did someone want her to notice and read it?

Maybe someone slipped it in while she worked. She was distressed to discover there were religious types here, too. They always seemed to want to fix her life. After what Rocky just told her, she thought he was probably the one who put the religious book in her drawer.

She picked up the Bible and turned it over in her hands. Could she really find some answers in this ancient book? Did God really write it, or direct someone to write it? She always thought it was a nice idea with some interesting stories, like David and Goliath. But it wasn't, in any stretch, attractive to her. She put it down to rest her head on a pillow.

A few hours later, she fixed a snack—sardines and cheddar cheese—her favorite. Listening to the news, she heard, "President John Kennedy promises U.S. troops to help Vietnam fight the northern communists. The president assured the American People these troops will only advise."

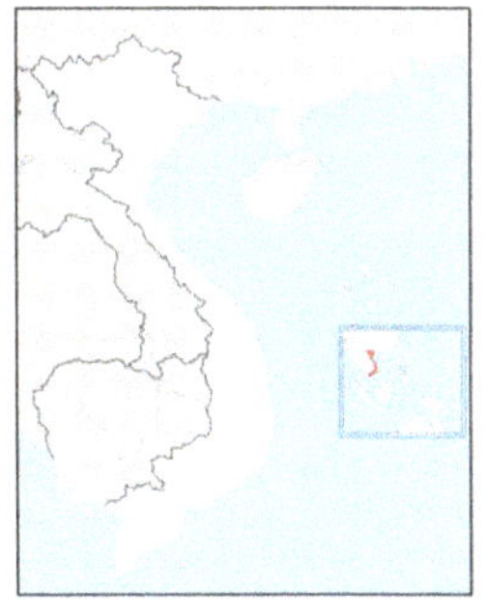

Knowing the Navy would soon call up Thomas, she felt she'd failed as a mother. Would he be involved? The Navy surely wouldn't send sailors to fight on land—or would they? She sighed, thinking of her kids. Still, she believed they were safer with Grandpa than they would be running from Vini the Fin.

She called Gloria, her high school friend, to find out if she knew anything about what was happening to

Thomas. She used the phone in the kitchen, "Hey Gloria, it's me." She avoided her real name, so she hoped Gloria would recognize her voice.

Gloria did, "Loretta, where are you? Are the kids okay? What are you doing?"

"Whoa, Girl. One question at a time. I'm okay. The kids are at Grandpa's. Here's my number—tell me anything I should know. Okay?" She hoped her attempt at motherhood would impress her high school friend.

Gloria tried to help Loretta see her errors, but hadn't succeeded. "I'll help, but you need help too—go to the police, stop running, seek God. He's the answer you REALLY need."

Loretta wasn't in the mood for another sermon. "See you later, girl. Keep safe and keep me informed. Bye." She hung up before Gloria could say more, leaving her best friend with prayer as the only recourse.

Tomorrow was her day off—Friday. Could she relax, with Vini the Fin still around? Would she be safe going out? Perhaps she would run into him again! Fear mixed with excitement as she prepared to do some sightseeing

Would she ever have a normal life? Was it ever normal? Her mind drifted to childhood—hard days cooking and cleaning for her father and brothers, Wally and Jackie.

She was only nine when her mother took off for the wild side of life, leaving her to fend for herself. She had to work hard to buy school clothes, and she never had time for sports or other extra-curricular activities.

She hated her mother for depriving her of a normal life. Abandoning the family was a horrible thing to do; it ruined Loretta's childhood. She had needed a mother to help her through the complex parts of adolescence. Even if her mother, Maude, had been home, she probably wouldn't have helped anyway, but it sure was worth trying for. At least this is what she thought now.

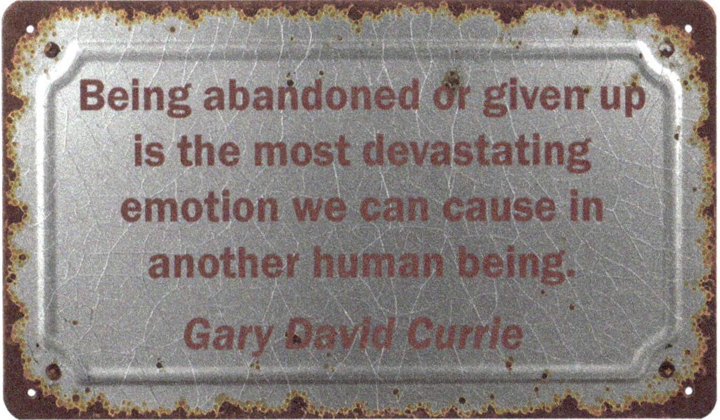

But, wait a minute, wasn't she doing the same thing to Kosette? Her God-given conscience was now revving up to full capacity, like a jet engine. WAS SHE DOING THE SAME THING TO KOSY? Really, was it the same thing or not? She rationalized that it wasn't, because if the kids were with her now, they'd be in danger too, just as she was.

So, they were really SAFER at Grandpa's farm. Now there, that settled it for the time being. Some would call her a hypocrite for thinking this way; others would write her off as a worthless mother or an unredeemable

addict. Whomever she actually was, there would be no change for the present.

She was just about to walk out of the restaurant for a day of R&R on the streets of San Francisco when Dwayne called her into the back. "There's a phone call for you." This was not good. Only one person knew where she was. She hoped with all her might this call came from that ONE person.

It wouldn't be good for anyone else to know of her whereabouts; it would actually be dangerous. Vini the Fin would do anything to anyone to find out where she was. With a lump in her throat, she put the receiver to her ear.

"Hey, Girl, what's this nonsense about being Linda Olson? I had a hard time convincing them it was actually you I wanted to talk to. You asked me to let you know what Thomas was doing. He's in San Diego at the Naval Training Center, boot camp. They called him the same day you left. Are you sure you don't want to contact your kids in Lacomb?"

Loretta's heart dropped a few beats from the race track speed it had been running at. "Well, I have to lie low. Changing my name is part of the scam. Thanks for the info on Thomas. Have you gotten any more calls from the people looking for me?" She hoped not. This is the best her unbelieving heart could come up with: hoping, crossing her fingers, and saying 'Oh my God,' which is the only time she ever used His name. "I have to go now, see you later."

Gloria wanted to talk more to find out what was going

on and where she was. When she called for Loretta instead of Linda, no one at the restaurant would give her any information about the location. All she could figure out from the area code was that Loretta was in the Bay Area.

Vini the Fin had made more phone calls to Gloria's house. He was not a pleasant person. His cursing and temper frightened her. She was very concerned for her family. Would this thug actually do something to harm her or her family because she wouldn't tell him where Loretta was? She wouldn't tell him even if she knew, and she didn't know.

Dwayne watched Linda during the whole phone conversation. He was not happy with her demeanor. She was hiding something. Why would someone call here asking for Loretta and then end up talking to Linda? Was it Linda who worked for him, or was it Loretta? He was determined to find out eventually. Today was her day off. She worked hard, so he decided to deal with the mystery later. He had enough experience to tell when someone was in desperate straits, and this young woman was certainly in that group.

San Francisco is one of the world's greatest tourist cities. WHY? Mainly because of the Golden Gate Bridge, Fisherman's Wharf, and the ancient cable cars. The cars are actually trolleys, operated by

a cable that runs under the steep hills. They are controlled by trolley men who use large levers to adjust the speed of descent and the force of climbing the streets, which are lined by picturesque houses like the 'Painted Ladies.'

The owners of these houses banded together to make them world famous in San Francisco, and it happened. They are called the 'Painted Ladies.'

Loretta was working only a few blocks from the end of the most famous cable car run. It took its eager tourists from all over the world to the restaurants and shops of the Wharf. This is precisely where she headed, "Finally, I'm going to ride the cable car. This should be a really great experience."

She bought a ticket. Holding onto the handrail, she jumped up the two steps. Some kind man gave her his seat. Loretta thought she had seen him somewhere else; at least his size and face seemed familiar. She just shook it off as a trick of the mind or a lack of good memory. She could hear the cable begin to move under the street.

The trolley man pulled forcefully back on the long lever, putting all his weight into the effort. The trolley jerked forward and started the sharp descent to the Wharf. It was going slow enough that other tourists could run alongside, grab the bar mounted on the side of the trolley, and swing aboard. They would pay at the end of the ride.

Loretta was enjoying the beautiful houses decorating both sides of the street. People here really took pride in their homes. Why not? They were on display to the whole world through the tourist industry. She cleared her mind of all distractions and just lost her soul in the beautiful, sunny San Francisco day.

Suddenly, she heard a loud crack, like a rifle shot. She noticed the trolley man fall to the floor with the lever smashed against his ample belly. It seemed as though the handle smacked him in the head, and he was out. "Great Scott," she yelped, "we're in free fall."

The man who gave her his seat moved quickly to grab the steering wheel because the trolley had jumped off the tracks. It was going to take some superhuman strength to drive it. Did this man think he could do it? Could any man do it?

What would he do to keep the trolley from dropping into the bay at the end of the run? He looked confident enough. He yelled, "Everyone, sit down and hold on tight."

He began to steer the trolley to the side of the street. It appeared his goal was to sideswipe every parked car.

He was going to make the auto shops in that area very rich. He smashed a few Buicks and Cadillacs, then went for the Fords and Chevys.

After he had exhausted all the autos on the right side of the street, he maneuvered the trolley to the other side, doing the same damage to the vehicles there. He was making progress; the trolley was slowing down. He shouted for everyone to jump off as soon as he gave them the thumbs up.

They were bug-eyed and reciting their prayers when he finally gave them the sign. Just as Loretta quickly sprang to her frightened, little feet to make a life-saving jump, he pointed to her and shouted, "Sit down, NOW."

For some reason, she didn't think it was wise to go against his command. She sat down. Now there were just the two of them on the runaway trolley. She didn't know why she obeyed him; he just seemed to have a commanding presence.

He was entirely in charge and knew exactly what needed to be done; he wasn't afraid to give orders. At the end of the run, the trolley busted through a few hippies' wares spread out on blankets, sending all the handmade earrings and bracelets flying in every direction. The vendors were running for their lives.

The busted-up trolley finally came to a screeching stop just ten feet from the bay. A few seagulls scurried off, and the sea lions barked at him. He did it; he was brave enough to do the job. He

wasn't staying around for handshakes, back slaps, and a medal ceremony.

Just before he stepped down, he turned to Loretta and looked her right in her relieved eyes, "You were saved this time, Loretta, now you need to look into saving your soul before it's too late. You may not survive the next adventure. Think about it."

And then he disappeared into the crowd. He was so tall she could still see him walking a block away. "What just happened?" she thought to herself. "Who was that man?" Goosebumps filled her forearms, and her hair stood up on the back of her neck.

This photo was taken in 1933.

John Franklin Taylor (Grandpa) standing with his three children, whom he was left to raise alone for nine years. Walter is to the left of Grandpa, and Jackie is on the right side of the photo. My mother, Loretta, is on the far left. She was only nine years old when her mother left and never came back.

Grandpa was a lumberjack at Snow Peak Lumber Company at this time. It was, and still is, located at the back of the farm.

2 - Bert the Bean Picker

A 1957 Chevrolet was a classic. It was the dream car of almost every young man. The style was certainly eye-catching. A two-door sedan was the classiest. A convertible was like having whipped cream on your strawberry shortcake.

Maybe in Minnesota, where Sergeant Kochian was from, a convertible wouldn't be appropriate. There, it drops to 70 below zero with the wind chill. In the Willamette Valley, where Shane lived, it freezes for only a few days in winter. Being caught with the top down during a sudden downpour is the worst thing that could happen.

Now that the strawberry and raspberry season was over, Shane and Kosy would work in the pole bean harvest. It would look a little strange—a fifteen-year-old driving a '57 Chevy to pick pole beans. It could be compared to a man driving his Rolls-Royce to pick up his welfare check. Shane had a very unusual situation.

He was joyfully pondering all of these recent blessings from God when he and Kosy returned to the farm and noticed Grandpa clearing a rather large patch of ground behind the house, closer to the river. They were curious and meandered over to find out what was going on.

They both grabbed a hoe and started clearing the weeds away. Kosy called out, "We can help, Grandpa. What's this going to be, another garden?" She hoped so; the veggies and fruit grown on the farm were eaten with great delight. When there was too much left over at the last harvest, Grandma Julia would either freeze it or can it.

Jack Woods never stopped for a minute. He kept on clearing the lot as he answered his granddaughter's question. "I always believed your mom would come home someday, come home to stay. That she will get saved, quit drinking and gambling, so you kids can have a mom and a home you've always deserved. So, I'm going to build a house here for you three to live in. A home of your own, right here beside ours."

Shane and Kosy were bug-eyed and dumbfounded, the weight of their grandfather's words leaving them momentarily frozen. Kosy found her voice first, hesitantly breaking the silence. "Grandpa, are you serious? Are we really going to have a home here, forever?" Her disbelief quickly turned to emotion, and tears welled up in her eyes as she began to wipe them away.

Shane was speechless. Shock washed over his face as his jaw dropped. He managed to say, "What a wonderful plan, Grandpa. We can help you, can't we? We want to help. But we're so flabbergasted, so absolutely shocked. This'll be a big project and will cost a lot of money. Money, we know you don't have. How are we going to pay for this?"

Before he answered their question, Jack led them into the house and opened an ancient jewelry box. "This is a cameo my great-great-grandmother passed down the family line. It was always to be given to the oldest daughter. I was planning on giving it to my only daughter at her graduation from high school.

"But she ran off with a boy none of us approved of. So this has been sitting here for 18 years, waiting for her to come back. I believe God is going to do something in her life, and she'll someday walk down that path out there and start being a good mother to you three. Then I'll give her this gift." This rough-and-tumble ex-lumberjack, and now diesel mechanic, had to fight back tears, which were becoming obvious to his two curious grandchildren.

The father never stopped loving his daughter. Since he accepted Christ, he'd never ceased to pray for her salvation. He also prayed for her return to his life and the farm. The grandfather loved his grandchildren and, now for the third time, had taken them in. He longed for the day when he could hug his daughter and she would never again leave his farm. Now they all prayed it would happen. God was mighty.

"Now, how are we going to pay for it? That's up to God. I believe we need this house, and He wants us to build it right here. I believe Philippians 4:19, which says, He will supply all our needs. So, we're going to pray and watch the money come in. How's that?"

Stroking his chin, Shane burst out, "I can't wait to explain all of this to Thomas. He'll be delighted to know what we're doing to help you with this wonderful project. Imagine that! We're going to have our own home, right here on Crabtree Creek, right next to Grandpa and Grandma. It'll be a little slice of heaven on earth. Then your farm won't be just a refuge for us, it'll be our permanent home." Both he and Kosy got goosebumps just thinking about it.

~~~~~~

No one knows why it happens, but just by observing life, one can't come to any other conclusion. Unfortunately, sometimes bad kids come from good parents. Likewise, good kids come from bad parents. It's not genetic; no one is born good or bad. How one turns out depends a lot on their upbringing. This is why it's very, very important for kids to have both a dad and a mom who love them, discipline them, and set a good example for them to follow. They need a moral compass and a rudder of integrity to keep them traveling down the right path.

~~~~~~

The Farnsworth family was quite well known in Lebanon. They tried hard to give their son, Engelbert, a good home and a 'religious' upbringing. They were always insisting that he study hard, work, and stay out of trouble. He wasn't cooperating. The only area in which he did a so-so job was his studies. He had to maintain a 'C' average, or he couldn't wrestle.

But the other two areas were not a concern to him. He was old enough to make his own decisions and choose his own friends. Now he was forced to work in the bean harvest because his dad said he had to buy his own gas.

Kosy came back from the water wagon at Doug Pederson's Pole Bean Farm. She whispered urgently, "You won't believe who I saw. He's going to pick the third row over from us. Old Engelbert 'the bully and brat' Farnsworth III, your bosom buddy!"

"I can't imagine a banker's son out here in this heat picking beans," Shane said aloud, pausing as he heard someone coming.

Kosy had been right. Engelbert Farnsworth III and his constant comrades were stomping down the row, just out of sight, but not out of sound.

"Hey Bert, are you sure you want to pick beans, like a migrant worker? Why it's so hot out here, you could melt," someone said sarcastically.

"Oh shut up, clod. My dad insists I work out here with the common people. He claims it'll build character," Bert responded disgustedly. Because of the rows of dense foliage between them, he didn't see the Woods duo.

"Did you notice the large bin where they pour the beans from our sacks is full?" Bert grinned maliciously. "That means they won't empty our sacks and give them back to us as usual. They'll have to stack them alongside the full bin and give us another sack. NOW is the time to hide some rocks in with our beans. We can make some extra wampum the easy way."

"Sure, Bert," one of his good buddies agreed. "Do you think there's a chance we could get caught? If not, I'm with you."

"He's got to be kidding," Kosy hissed to Shane. "He's going to steal Mr. Pederson's hard-earned money by putting rocks in with the beans. I'm not going to let him get by with this. Where's Grandma?" Julia Woods was a row boss. It was her job to check whether all the beans ready for harvest were actually picked. If they weren't, the unhappy worker would have to pick the whole row again.

After Grandma was informed, she warned the weighers. When good old Engelbert Farnsworth III showed up with a large sack of beans, it was weighed. "It looks like 125 pounds," the weigher smirked at the picker. "Kind of heavy, huh, Kid?"

Bert tried to look nonchalantly innocent. "I guess the gunny sack must be really wet," he said, feigning ignorance.

The weigher was grinning when he pointed to the back of the large bin, "Just dump the sack over there behind the bin."

Bert looked uncomfortable now. He began chewing nervously on his lower lip. "What's the matter? What's the big deal? You aren't dumping the sacks of the other pickers. What's going on? Don't you trust me?" he protested.

"Oh sure, we trust you, Bert," the weigher shot back

with a smirk. "We trust you about as far as we can throw you. Let's just say we don't have rocks in our heads." When they dumped the beans on the ground, two stones, about the size of softballs, rolled out.

"Well, looky here," the weigher faked a look of surprise. "Some extra weight to give you a little more gas money, huh, Bert? You must have one oar in the water if you think we're fooled so easily. Hit the road, Kid. You can't work here anymore. You're fired. Now go home and tell your daddy and mommy. I can't wait until you see their reaction. I'd love to be a fly on the wall in that room."

As he was packing his lunch into the car, Bert was beside himself. He was so livid, everyone there could imagine he had smoke coming out of his ears. "How in the world could they possibly have known about the rocks?"

Kosy and Shane just smiled at each other as they watched the teenage crook drive out of the parking lot. Shane remarked, "He won't be cheating Mr. Pederson anymore."

"That's for sure," Kosy replied, joining him. "By the way, I'm sure glad it's Friday. I'm looking forward to a few days off. When I close my eyes at night, all I see is rows of unpicked pole beans. It wouldn't be quite a nightmare if it were a row of picked pole beans."

The first day of school was only three weeks away.

Shane was enjoying his summer. The Lord had really been changing his life. He greabbed his Bible to leave for church. "Kosy, what a lovely dress you're wearing. I've never seen you dressed so nicely," he complimented.

"With this new dress Erin helped me pick out, maybe I can be a different person," Kosy thought. "Possibly, I can even impress someone at church. Right now, there's nowhere else to wear it. If I can change enough, maybe God will look at me differently, maybe He'll let me into His heaven."

"Thanks, Shane," Kosy responded proudly. "I hope my new clothes will make a difference in my life. I know I need to be a better person."

That morning, Kosy's Sunday School teacher, Mrs. Lillian Payne, taught about Joshua and the battle of Jericho. It seemed as though she was talking directly to Kosy. "God doesn't look on our outward appearances as man does. He knows our hearts. Is your heart right before God? If not, you need to accept Christ as your Savior today."

In the morning service that followed, Pastor Ballentine preached on Revelation 20:11-15. "The final judgment will come someday. If you've never received Jesus Christ as your Savior, you're not saved and won't pass through the Pearly Gates. There will be no place in heaven for you. You're not prepared to die! Do you want to find your name written in the Lamb's Book of Life?"

The pastor read a verse that really touched Kosy's

heart. "And whosoever was not found written in the  book of life was cast into the lake of fire." Kosy was finally paying attention, really CLOSE attention. She didn't exactly understand what "the Lake of Fire" meant but it sounded like someplace she REALLY didn't want to go.

At the invitation, she grabbed the pew in front of her and held on until her knuckles turned white. Shane was observing the whole struggle. He leaned towards Kosy and whispered in her ear, "Quit fighting God, Kosy. If you want to accept Christ, I'll go forward with you, okay?"

With that coaxing, Kosy let go of the pew. Shane grabbed her by the hand and walked to the front of the church with her. When Pastor Ballentine asked why they had come, Shane answered for them, "I'm bringing my sister to Christ. She needs to be saved."

Mrs. Ballentine talked to her, "Are you really serious about accepting Christ, Kosy?"

"Yes, Mrs. Ballentine," Kosy said, her eyes moist. "I realize I'm a sinner and Christ is the Savior. I don't want to pay the price of my sin. I want Jesus to be MY Savior, like Shane did. I want nothing to do with any Lake of Fire."

Marva Ballentine took Kosy to a side room and showed her some verses. The abandoned eleven-year-old asked to pray.

"Lord of Shane and Erin, I noticed how much my brother's life has changed, and I love that. You know how much I've hated our mom for leaving us and making jailbirds out of us. I know I've sinned, and this sin is going to keep me out of heaven. I ask Jesus, Your Son, to come into my heart and save me now. I want to spend eternity with You and my friends here. Thank You, Lord, for saving me. Amen."

After the service, the whole church family rejoiced as their many prayers were finally answered. Marty commented, "Now we need to continue praying for Thomas, and for Mrs. Woods, Kosy's mom."

Erin gave Kosy a big hug. "I'm so happy for you, Kosy. Why don't we celebrate? Let's get our swimsuits and head into town. We can grab a hamburger at the Tastee Freeze and then go swimming." She glanced at Shane with a friendly wink.

"How about the Waterloo Bridge?" Shane suggested. "Have you swum there yet? That's the other famous bridge in Linn County."

A gravel-road shortcut via the New Berlin Pass would take Shane to the Waterloo Bridge. But anyone driving a 1957 Chevy convertible would want to avoid bouncing rocks off its frame. They wisely decided against the shortcut. Besides, it didn't take them past the Tastee Freeze Drive-in in Lebanon.

To get to the swimming hole from the drive-in, Shane had to take Santiam Highway and go through Waterloo. Waterloo is a berg, only a little wider spot in the road than Lacomb. Kosy realized how small it was, "Don't blink your eyes when you pass through, or you'll miss it entirely." Oregon is peppered with little towns like Waterloo. Many of them are located next to water, too. It made Oregon boast of a good life that only one in a million people experienced.

Sometimes people get brave enough to jump off the high Waterloo Bridge; after all, it's only fifty feet to the water's edge. Those who do jump go feet first. No one would be foolish enough to dive headfirst. The water is plenty deep, the current quick.

Young swimmers like to brag about swimming the one hundred yards across the river. If a swimmer wants to arrive at the short beach on the Waterloo side, he has to start quite a ways upstream. The current is swift enough to carry even good swimmers right past the beach and into the rocky rapids.

Marty was backing up into the water. Just as Shane began to say, "There's a drop off right behind y ..." Marty disappeared under the bubbles.

When he finally came up, blowing water like a whale, he chided Shane, "Why didn't you tell me before I went down?"

"Well, for one thing, I tried to, and for the other—you never asked!"

The rope swing fastened to the bottom of the bridge was long, allowing for a wide sweep, ending in some good dives. Some were brave enough or foolish enough to try a swan dive.

Shane was swinging back and forth, getting enough distance for his dive. Kosy had not recovered completely from her near drowning, so she wasn't about to try a rope swing just yet. She sat with her feet in the water, skipping rocks halfway across the river.

She was only eleven years old, but had so many experiences—some good, but mostly bad. The years with mom were mostly bad; bouncing from boarding home to boarding home while Loretta was on her frequent drinking sprees. These memories made her shake her head in sorrow. She was sure those days were all behind her now that she was living with Jack and Julia Woods, on their wonderful farm.

Suddenly, Kosy reared back her head and wrinkled up her nose. She sneezed three times in rapid-fire succession. Standing up, she took a quick survey of the area and soon discovered the reason for her allergies. She yelled at Shane, "Hey, Ape Man, I've got bad news for us. My allergies to smoke have attacked again."

To everyone's applause and with a Tarzan yell, Shane did a small swan dive into the clear, cool water. They expected him to come up immediately. He delayed, twenty seconds, thirty seconds, forty, and still counting … Just as Marty was about to begin a rescue operation, Shane's head broke water.

"Look, I've got a set of keys," Shane yelled as he gasped for breath. He held up the key chain. "There's a jeep down there. It looks almost new with just a little rust. The keys were still in the ignition."

"Oh, sure, and I suppose you shut the motor off when you took the keys. Did you also roll up the windows?" Erin wasn't going to fall for any of Shane's tricks. "This isn't April first, you know. Was the motor flooded?"

"No, seriously, there's a Willys Jeep down there. You can just make out the frame if you look hard enough. See, right there," Shane insisted, as he pointed to a dark shadow in the deeper area.

"Okay, so you weren't kidding," Erin apologized. "What's a jeep doing down there with the keys in the ignition?"

Shane was as dumbfounded as she was. "How could I possibly know that? I suggest we dive down, get the license number, and then talk to Sergeant Kochian."

On the way back home, Shane stopped at the police headquarters. The radio was squeaking as usual. They entered Sergeant Kochian's office. It was a hunter's paradise. On the back wall hung a mounted head of a large buck.

Shane was impressed. "How much did that buck weigh?" Kosy wanted to know how fast the buck was running when it hit the outside wall, forcing its head through to hang on the inside wall. No one answered her question. She went outside to see the other end of the buck.

"About three hundred pounds, dressed out," Sergeant Kochian responded proudly. "It took three of us to haul it out of Snow Peak Wilderness."

On the other side of the room was a stuffed mountain lion. Kosy had returned from outside and was running her hand down the back of the puma. "It looks almost real, like it could bite me. Did YOU shoot this mountain lion? There aren't many around here anymore."

Sergeant Kochian liked Kosy. "My Little Friend, that particular mountain lion was killing sheep out by Scio. I was obligated to hunt it down. I shot it with my bow."

"Don't tell me you also shot this bison in Linn County?" Marty questioned.

"No, that was a gift from a Native American friend in North Dakota. What can I do to help you kids? I know you didn't come by here to admire the wildlife or to have a biology or history lesson."

Shane explained their discovery. "We were swimming

at the Waterloo Bridge, and I found a Willys Jeep right under the rope swing. We were wondering if you might be able to find the owner by the license plate number?"

"I can do better than that," the sergeant promised. "I chased that stolen jeep all over the countryside out by Waterloo. There was a poached deer in the back. They threw some nails on the road that blew out my tires and they got away. Those miserable poachers must've driven it off the bank at the Waterloo Bridge."

"Yeah, and when Shane found it, the motor was still running," Kosy giggled.

Sergeant Kochian raised his eyebrows at Kosy. "You, my friend, have been hanging around this circus troop too long."

Marty wanted more information. "Whose jeep is it?"

"It was stolen from Gerlach Motors. Let me call them right now and see what Mr. Gerlach wants to do about it."

As he listened to Sergeant Kochian talk to the business owner, Shane admired the mounted pink salmon on the wall. "He even likes to fish. This is my kind of man!"

The sergeant put down the phone. "They said their insurance already paid for the jeep. As far as they and the insurance company were concerned, because it was submerged in water, both agreed to change the claim from 'stolen' to 'total loss.' So, the first one to drag it out of the river can have it."

At that, Shane bid Sergeant Kochian goodbye and headed for the T.P. Oil Company. "Bowie, can your dad's tow truck pull a jeep from the bottom of the river at the Waterloo Bridge?"

"What have you been doing, Shane, driving with your eyes closed again?" Bowie couldn't help but rib his friend, whom he liked so much. "Sure, we can. Why, if you hook up enough pulleys, you could lift almost anything."

With a set of pulleys, the jeep was recovered to the surprise of all the swimmers who were watching, and to the joy of the Lacomb junior detectives.

"All we have to do now is dry it out and change the wiring," Shane calculated. "Possibly the carburetor and gas tank will need to be replaced, or thoroughly broken down and cleaned piece by piece. If there's any water in the block, we'll have to pull the head and replace the rings. No big deal though."

On the hillside overlooking the rescue operation, three very angry, unhappy, scowling poachers clenched their fists in anger! They vowed on their mother's coffin that they would get even with these do-gooders if it was the last thing they would ever do. It might very well be, too.

3 - Learning to Witness

Poaching is a common problem in Linn County. White-tailed deer and rainbow trout are the usual targets. If a doe is killed in the spring or early summer, there will usually be a fawn that will die of starvation or fall victim to predators. 

Regular hunting season begins at the end of September and usually lasts for six weeks. Anything shot out of season is considered poaching. Violators are heavily fined, and some even go to jail. Most poachers kill for their own use, while others make a business out of the illegal slaughter.

Shane disliked poachers with a passion. "There's no way three game wardens for this area can keep the poaching under strict surveillance. There are about 700 square miles of the Snow Peak Wilderness. Maybe 50 game wardens could make a difference, but just three is a joke—only the poachers are laughing. Most poachers know that, and they have full run of the acreage. This is appalling."

Erin, frustrated, turned to Shane. "Can't anyone hear

the shots and report them? Something has to be done. What can we do?" Erin always wanted solutions—now.

Shane knew a lot about poachers. "Most poachers use a light rifle, like a .22, with short, quiet bullets. The shot sounds like a twig cracking. They usually only shoot once, making it almost impossible to get a bearing on them. During the regular season, hunters use bigger guns, a 30.06 or 30.30.

"Remember the guy who fell off the electric pole near your house? I saw blood on his car—maybe from putting a deer in the trunk. We should keep an eye on that crowd."

Marty entered the Lynch living room with a big bowl of popcorn, shifting the conversation away from poaching to their ongoing mechanical project. "Do you think we can get that Willys Jeep running? We've already pulled the head and cleaned all the moving parts, including the rods and bearings. We still have all the rewiring to do."

"Sure, we can get it going," Shane encouraged the obviously inexperienced mechanic. "My grandfather has had lots of years working with four-cylinder engines. Once, he bought a Japanese jeep that had been used in World War II. It had a small V-2 engine. Those Japanese were so economical, they used only one piston, and it swapped holes."

"Really," Erin queried, "That's amazing!"

"If you believe that," Marty grinned, "I have some lovely seaside property in Arizona to sell you."

"Fine, Shane, no popcorn for you. Instead, a pillow in the face!" Erin hurled pillows at him, demonstrating her love of playful banter and doing something memorable with Shane.

Marty was still thinking about Shane's story. "Well, no wonder they lost the war. They were using motorcycle engines in their jeeps. Come on, Shane, let's leave before you get hurt. I want to practice some wrestling moves. I expect to wrestle in an AAU tournament in Corvallis next weekend."

"You mean before YOU hurt me on the mat? What's this wrestling tournament in Corvallis?"

"Would you like to come along? There will be some awesome wrestlers there. It could be a great place to see both skilled wrestling and to look for opportunities to witness to others, which is something I'm passionate about alongside my interest in wrestling.

"Shane, did you know wrestling mats are so cushiony you can drop an egg from a stepladder without breaking it?"

"Let's try it. Sounds fun." Shane said.

On the way to the wrestling room, Marty grabbed two eggs. "Let's try. You clean up if it fails, Erin."

"Okay, no problem, I've seen this trick work before."

After placing a protective cover on the mat, they positioned the ladder. Marty climbed to the top. "Here goes nothing." He dropped an egg. It bounced around a little but didn't break. Even upon a minute investigation by 'Hawkeye Shane,' not even one slight crack was found.

Following his examination of the egg, Shane threw it on the mat as hard as he could, smashing it. "Too bad, Erin. The yolk's on you! Time to clean up."

After SHANE thoroughly cleaned all traces of the egg off the mat, the real action started. Three minutes of intense wrestling is enough to tire anyone. Marty was in shape—Shane wasn't. Marty couldn't let it go by. "You're not in bad shape for the shape you're in." One was chuckling while the other was trying to force a weak but tired smile through his deep panting.

"I run five miles a day. Great for endurance, rough on my knees. I'd rather wrestle," Marty said.

Shane lay back, panting. "Once I can breathe, I'll ask you something...Should I enter the AAU tournament?"

"You're not ready, Shane. You can enter, but you'll get wrapped up tight. These wrestlers are world-class. I don't expect to win any medals at this tournament.

"I'll enjoy the experience and probably even learn

something. We'll get to see some of America's greatest wrestlers. Rick Sanders from Portland State will be there. He's a national champion at 118 pounds."

"After today, it's just fruit and a few candy bars for me. I have to weigh-in a couple of hours before the meet starts. They give you a five-pound grace allowance. That means I can weigh in at 155 pounds if I want to wrestle at the 150-pound weight class."

"If you're trying to lose weight, why eat a candy bar?" Shane asked.

Marty threw Shane a Snickers bar. "Look at the weight."

Shane read the wrapper. "It looks like 1.8 ounces, so what?"

"How could you gain more than that? Three hundred calories and lots of protein."

Shane took a bite. "I don't want you overweight. About witnessing—what's involved?"

"Well, usually I take some good tracts along with me, like *God's Simple Plan of Salvation*. Since these wrestling tournaments attract many people, it's also a chance for me to witness, if God gives me

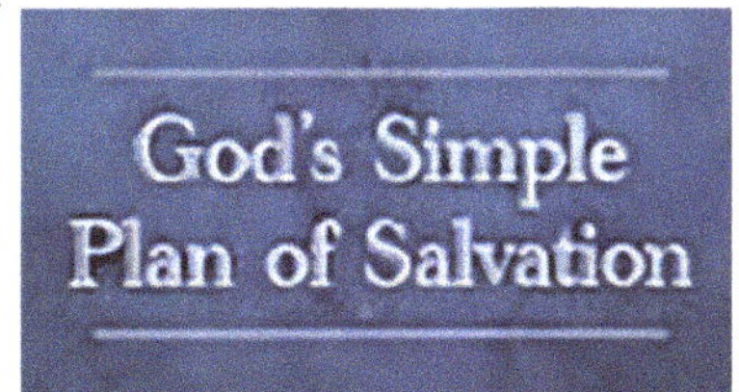

the opportunity. I ask a question or two and see where the conversation goes."

"What kind of question?" Shane asked, curious but nervous about being so bold in public.

Marty warmed up. "If you're bold, you ask, 'If you died today, do you know where you'd spend eternity?' or something similar."

"That's bold. I don't know if I'm ready to confront someone like that."

Marty continued, "If you're timid, ask, 'Are you interested in spiritual things?' It's an easier start."

"I'm not sure I can ask those questions," Shane admitted.

"It's just like wrestling," Marty explained. "The more you do it, the better you get. Shane, you have to be willing to try, and let God work out the details. I got a very slow start, with a timid approach, and worked my way to being bolder. It takes time, like most good things in life."

It was back to pushing weight around on the mat. Shane had already learned the single-leg takedown. He was now trying to master it. If he missed the knee, he wouldn't back off like

Some great wrestlers, especially brothers, have a room like this at home to get more practice hours.

some wrestlers. He would strike again, even surprising Marty.

That was the aggressive kind of wrestling Marty had taught him to do. "You're vulnerable when you're backing up. Always go sideways or forward."

After the hour workout, the scene shifted from the wrestling mat to the weight room for more training. A thick carpet decorated the small, well-lit room. When Marty had to drop something on the floor for lack of strength or a painful cramp, the collision wouldn't shake the rafters.

Erin was putting the saddle on Trapper when she saw two sweaty and tired wrestlers come out of the weight room. She smiled at Shane and mounted the horse. Soon, she was riding on an empty gravel road near the house.

She found herself attracted to this young Christian from California. Erin had been saved when she was four years old. Because her parents had raised her in the church, she had a good background of Bible knowledge and Christian conduct.

Shane had accepted Christ only a month ago, and he was making excellent progress. Would this California boy really be interested in a cowgirl from Montana, whose whole heart and life were dedicated to serving Jesus Christ? All these thoughts occupied her mind as she enjoyed the clean air sweeping down from Buzzard Butte.

Trapper trotted up the road in the third lane, leaving

two lanes for cars to pass. Erin contemplated to herself, "Just being a Christian isn't enough." She had seen her share of mediocre Christians. She didn't want to be like that. Her goal in life was to give herself completely to the Savior, without reservation. Being totally dedicated to the Son of God only seemed logical. Hadn't Jesus Christ given His all for her?

Mediocrity made her sick to her stomach. Apparently, the Lord had the same reaction to it. She had just read that morning about the Lord's feelings toward lukewarmness. "Where was that passage? II Peter, no. I remember now! It was Revelation 3:15-16. Jesus said He would rather a person be cold than lukewarm. That's really interesting. I'll have to talk to Pastor Ballentine about that."

She was willing to serve anywhere, in any capacity, even if it meant full-time missionary service at the end of the earth. She wasn't giving anything less than her all to the Master. Life would mean nothing serving herself. Would Shane understand all this? Could he also be that totally dedicated?

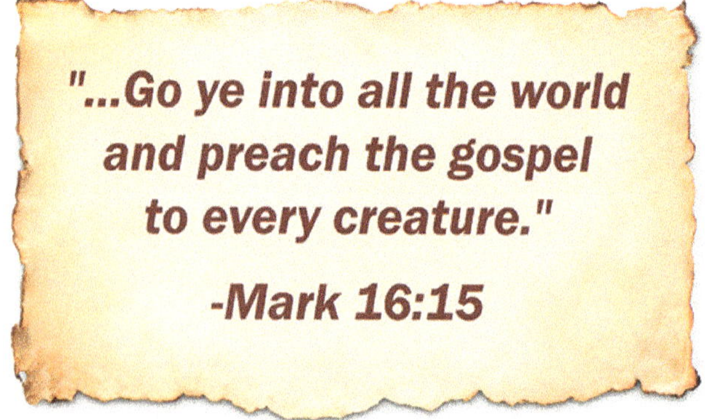

Even though she liked Shane, Erin would never consider a serious relationship unless he was totally dedicated to Christ. No secret discipleship would do. Shane would have to be public about his devotion to the Savior. If Shane were embarrassed to take a stand for Christ at school, then he'd certainly not be the kind of person she'd want to date.

She turned Trapper off the road and started up a logging trail. "Let's stop here, Trapper. I want to pray." Right there, surrounded by God's creation and awed by it all, Erin Lynch, a tenderhearted teenage girl, sold out to Christ, bowed her head, and entered the Throne of Grace.

"Oh God, I come into Your presence in the name of Your Son, Jesus Christ. Please give Shane the same desires I have. I certainly wouldn't miss Your will for any good-looking blond from California. And by the way, Lord, I'd like to see some evidence of this very commitment soon. I ask this because, as you know, I'm a very impatient person."

Now and then, she liked a solitary ride. She wanted to think about her future and enjoy God's creation. It was always fun with the others, usually a circus or an adventure, but sometimes it was good to be alone.

Rain had been abundant lately, making the wild grass exceptionally green and tall. A robin was dipping and diving while chasing a sparrow. A nearby chipmunk ran wildly up and down a branch, scolding them both.

Suddenly, Trapper's front hoof slipped into a groundhog

hole, and Erin went flying off to the right, hitting her head solidly on the ground. When she came to, about five minutes later, there was a strange, bearded, smelly man blowing his horrible breath right in her face.

4 - First Wrestling Tourney

"What happened?" Erin stammered, pressing her hand to her head wound. She brushed back the older man with the tattered beard, surprised to find him only inches from her nose, his breath filling the air between them with horrible smells. "Who are you, and how did you get here so quickly?"

"Well, you've certainly got a lot of questions, Missy" he replied as he helped her to her feet, giving her a quick look over. "Glad you came to. I didn't think you'd want me to give you mouth-to-mouth, since I chew tobacco. I'll help you get on your horse and lead you to the road."

Erin shuddered at the thought of mouth-to-mouth resuscitation. He helped her mount Trapper, steadying the horse before leading them down the trail. With the reins in hand, he guided Trapper slowly, making sure Erin was secure. He stayed close until they reached the Rocking L Ranch entrance. There, he handed her the reins and, wordless, walked into the woods, disappearing as quickly as he'd appeared. Moments later, Erin was at the house, where the commotion of her return began.

There was a flurry of activity as Erin entered the house, blood trailing down her head and neck. Mr. Lynch cleaned the wound. "It looks worse than it is. Just a scrape. Some hydrogen peroxide, Mercurochrome, and plenty of TLC, and you'll be fine."

Shane was patting Erin on the shoulder. "You'll be okay, girl. By the way, what's TLC?"

The whole Lynch family looked at Shane in disbelief. Mr. Lynch thought, "This kid needs a lot of it." Aloud, he said, "It means 'tender loving care.' We have plenty of it here, right, Erin?"

"Right, Dad. That man was strange, Mom. He was breathing right in my face. I could smell his breath, a mixture of garlic and tobacco."

"He was probably checking to see if you were still breathing," Shane informed them all. "He was a medical corpsman in the Korean Conflict."

"You know him?" Mrs. Lynch asked as she put the first aid kit back in the medicine cabinet.

"Not really," Shane answered quickly. "Nobody actually KNOWS him. We only know ABOUT him."

"Well, tell us what you know. He sounds like an interesting person," Mr. Lynch commented. "Maybe we can invite him here to our home."

"I doubt he'd come, Mrs. Lynch," Shane said. "He's a hermit. From what I've heard, he saw a lot of action as a Navy nurse, or corpsman, in the Korean Conflict.

The violence stayed with him, and when he was discharged, he moved to Buzzard Butte. He's lived mostly alone ever since."

Marty was very interested in this new neighbor. "Well, does he at least have a name?"

"I'm sure he has a real name, but I don't know what it is. We call him Willy Evershave," Shane said, grinning as he stroked his chin in imitation of a beard. "Some say he pans for gold on the far side of Buzzard Butte in Snow Peak Wilderness."

"I bet his first name is Bill," Erin said. "Evershave is probably just a nickname because of his long beard, you know, like 'will he ever shave.' It's not hard to figure out. You don't have to be a detective to see that."

"You've probably seen him more than anyone else in the last few years." Shane was trying to put the whole thing into perspective.

"Yeah," Erin complained as she touched her head wound, "and I didn't even get a chance to thank him."

Marty enjoyed teasing his sister. "Did he leave a silver bullet in your hand? Did he wear a black mask? Did he ride off on a silver horse? Did he have a sidekick named Tonto?"

"Seriously, Marty, I do want to meet him again. He'd probably be as interested as we are in catching those poachers," Erin reasoned. "And he must be lonely. I always feel for people like that—those who are rejected or alone."

Meanwhile, as Erin and her family discussed their strange encounter, Marty focused on the AAU tournament and trained hard with Shane. He knew he gained little from wrestling his inexperienced neighbor, who only knew what Marty had taught him. Still, Shane was a body to practice with. The Californian was showing some improvement. He wasn't the pushover he had been and could now wrestle for thirty minutes with only short breaks.

"Why don't we get Bowie to come out here and wrestle with us?" Shane volunteered.

"Are you nuts, Shane? Bowie weighs almost as much as both of us combined. If he fell on us, we'd be pancakes. He's a bone breaker. We need opponents close to our own size to avoid injury. One pulled muscle and you're out half a season; a broken bone, and it's wait until next year."

"Okay, Marty, you made your point," Shane conceded. "Now, what time shall we pick you up to leave for Corvallis?"

"Weigh-in is at 7:00 AM. How about five o'clock?"

"Good grief, Marty," Shane complained. "I'll have to get up before breakfast to get here that early!"

The morning of the tournament arrived quickly. The '57 convertible pulled into Rocking L Ranch at 5:00 AM. The roosters were warming up. Marty and Erin were coming out of the front of the house, rubbing their eyes. Kosy rolled down the window. "The early bird gets the worm."

"Thanks anyway, Kosy, but I've already had breakfast. I've heard the early bird gets the worm, but I also know it's the second mouse that gets the cheese." Erin answered tersely. "Our parents will be coming later, at a more civilized time, probably after the roosters wake up the hens."

Shane thought he'd add to the post-breakfast humor. "I know the early bird gets the worm, but what does the early worm get? Nothing but served up on the early bird's breakfast plate."

After the long drive, anticipation mounted as Shane

pulled onto the Oregon State Campus. He began his tour guide speech, "Welcome to the campus of Oregon State. This school of higher learning was founded nine years BEFORE Chief Joseph led his people in their famous escape attempt to the Canadian border. Until the present, Oregon State has no great claim to fame, but I haven't attended here yet."

A chorus of boos echoed throughout the parking lot. Shane wanted to have the last word. "Oregon State has all the classes you'll ever want to take and some you won't want to take, like Quantum Physics. Just sign up at the field house."

Marty weighed in, taking Shane with him. In the locker room, parading around the scale, were modern-day gladiators. They all had hungry looks in their eyes. Some had been at this sport for twenty years.

They thrived on competition and survived on lettuce washed down with protein drinks. They were friendly when they shook hands, but on the mat, their feigned friendliness would instantly morph into a fighting spirit. Wrestling ran in their blood.

Kosy and Erin waited at the front gate. Shane joined them after Marty had topped the scale at exactly 155 pounds. "That brother of yours really knows how to lose weight. He put the scale pin very close to the edge of what was allowed. Wow, it was close! I thought he was going to be overweight."

"Marty, overweight, you've got to be kidding," Erin bragged about her brother. "He's been doing this for years. He knows exactly what's needed to make the weight. He's never failed to make weight at a weigh-in, not even once! He weighs the lettuce and the fruit he eats and weighs himself three times a day."

Shane paid for Erin and Kosy's tickets. The cute redhead from Montana leaned over, close to Shane's face, and showed him a smile as wide as the desert horizon. "Well, since you paid for my ticket, does this constitute our first date, Shane?"

Erin smiled as she schemed, "And, since you paid for my ticket, I'll convince Marty to pay for our lunch, since he won't be needing any food himself."

A one-day wrestling tournament must be very well organized. There are ten weight divisions and various age groups. Over three hundred wrestlers could compete. Finals are at 8:00 PM. Each wrestler could have three to five matches, depending on how many wins they had.

The Oregon State basketball floor held eight mats,

"Where should we sit, Erin?" Kosy asked. "We'll want to get a close view of all Marty's matches. We can even take some action shots with Grandpa's camera."

Erin threw her hands up in the air. "Look, Kosy, there are eight mats. Marty could wrestle on any one of them, so we won't know where until they call his name and mat number. We'll be moving all over the gym before the day's through." With that, they both began scanning for seats and settled in to wait for Marty's announcement.

An open tournament means anyone could come. Each wrestler, aged 7 to 30, had their own singlet (wrestling uniform). Each tournament was a convention of narrow-waisted, broad-shouldered athletes. Few sports use weight as a criterion: combat sports (wrestling, boxing, and martial arts), weightlifting, rowing, some youth sports, and horse racing (for the jockey).

Wrestlers are always trying to compete in the lowest weight class possible, conserving as much strength as possible. There's a point in losing weight at which a wrestler could injure their health and lose strength. Marty was never interested in that kind of foolishness.

Each match consisted of three two-minute rounds. Marty entered the circle to face his first opponent. He shook hands with the Sweet Home High School student. They both began slowly, circling, watching, grabbing, and pulling.

Then, like lightning, Marty had the kid's right knee locked in tight. Marty pushed backwards, tripping the kid's left foot. Take-down, two points. The Marty Lynch fan club went wild.

Shane wanted to yell out some instructions, but held back, "Certainly, he knows more than I do. Just hang on, Marty."

Marty won his first match 6-4 and would have an hour break before his next one—a wrestler from Portland State. "He'll probably be my Waterloo," Marty commented, making a face. "He has six years more experience than I do."

The French emperor/general Napoleon was soundly defeated by the English general Wellington at the Battle of Waterloo. So, the phrase 'my Waterloo' has long been a classic for defining the defeat or likely defeat of anyone!

Shane thought Marty should be more optimistic. "Come on, Grappler, you can be more positive than that, can't you?"

"Shane, I know my abilities. At my stage of development, there's no way I could beat a wrestler from Portland State. Someday I'll be able to, but not yet. That's not being overly pessimistic, just realistic."

Shane noticed a mountain of a man standing on a mat

at the other side of the gym. "Who's that giant?"

Marty looked to where Shane had pointed. "That's America's biggest amateur wrestler, Chris Nelson, from Iowa."

"Big," Shane echoed, "he's not just big, he's a mountain on legs—a regular two-legged elephant! Good grief, he's twice as big as Bowie. How much does he weigh?"

"Well, since it's obvious he's a super heavyweight, he doesn't really have to weigh in," Marty explained. "Just for the record's sake, he goes to the meat locker and hangs on the hooks. That's the only scale capable of weighing him. Let's go over and give him a tract."

Shane's legs got a little weak; his knees started getting to know each other. He scratched his head. "What ... what are you going to say to him, Marty?"

"Nothing!" Marty handed Shane a tract. "I thought you'd get a chance to use what we've been practicing at my home, remember?"

"Okay, but I want Erin to come with me for moral support."

"We'll all go together," Marty insisted, "but you can give him the tract, all right?"

Shane walked up to Chris Nelson, noticing the rows of sweat warts on his neck. When Chris looked down at him, Shane felt like a grape about to be stomped on by a dinosaur. He handed a tract to Chris and started in what he had hoped was a confident voice, "I'm ... ah ... I'm Shane Woods, and I'd like to give you this to read. Do you know for sure where you'd spend eternity if you were to die today?" Whew, was he glad he was able to spit that out. He hoped the mountain of a man wouldn't be angry.

Chris took the little piece of paper in his huge hand that was as big as an eight-ounce professional boxing glove. "Well, thank you, my Little Friend. I have too many plans to do and too many places to go to start talking about dying. I still have the World Games and the Olympics to go to. Are you a religious person, Shane? What a dumb question! You must be, or you wouldn't be handing me this religious piece of paper."

"Well, I'm not really interested in religion," Shane answered. "That's a big ball of confusion. I don't really know much yet. But I do know that religion will never give anyone eternal life. Salvation is in a Person— Jesus Christ, not in a system or religion." Chris was somewhat friendly, so Shane got braver, "Will you read the tract, Chris?"

"Sure, Shane, my Little Buddy. Are you a wrestler, too?"

"I'm trying to be," Shane maintained stoutly. "I hope I never have to wrestle you."

Chris was amused at this pint-sized evangelist. "You'd have to eat a lot more pizzas and potatoes to wrestle me." And with that, Chris waddled away, chuckling to himself. Shane had survived his first live-witnessing attempt, and he was still intact!

Even though Marty was already psyched out before he stepped on the mat with the Portland State wrestler, he still managed to get the first takedown, a duck under, and a backward trip. A reversal followed, with Marty getting pinned in the first period.

His fan club was still vocally supporting him, even though Marty was counting the lights. He did manage to give the winner a tract. That was his usual practice, even when he lost.

Marty tied his next match, followed by an 8-7 win. He was still in the tournament until he lost his final match 6-1 to a wrestler from San Francisco State.

This is one of the few photos I have of me wrestling at Pillsbury Baptist Bible College in 1967. I always had the most pins on the team. We were always conference champs, too.

5 - Following a Poacher

"I knew I wouldn't win, Shane. It was worth the experience, though," Marty reasoned as they drove out of the Oregon State parking lot. "Some of those wrestlers are world-class, and I want to push myself against the best. Someday, if I keep working hard, maybe I'll be up to their level. I have my sights on the 1968 Olympics in Mexico City."

"Wow," Shane burst out, "do you think I could work on that goal, too? I'd have to really bear down, wouldn't I? I've always liked the phrase 'Good, better, best' I'll never rest until my good is better and my better is best."

"Sure, it'd take a lot of dedication, but you could do it. Dad and Mom told us to meet them at the T&R Truck Stop in Albany for hamburgers and cherry Cokes. Sounds good, huh?"

From Albany to Lebanon, the discussion turned to the day's BIG event. Shane opened the subject, "Did you see Chris Nelson wrestle? No one can move all that muscle and lard around on the mat. I wonder how much he weighed when he was born?"

"I read an article about him in *Sports Illustrated*," Marty chimed in. "They said he weighed thirteen pounds at birth, and before he entered junior high, he was up to 200 pounds. I sure wouldn't have liked to pay his food bills. He weighs more than 400 pounds now."

Erin beamed with pride, her heart pounding for Shane's courage. "Do you really think he'll read it, Marty? That little tract seemed lost in his giant hand," she said, her voice tremulous with hope.

"Who knows, Sis, maybe he will, and maybe he won't. Perhaps he'll throw it in the trash. We do our part and leave the rest up to God. There are some fantastic stories about people getting saved by just reading a tract someone gave them. Sometimes they don't get saved until years later."

Shane's uncertainty gnawed at him; he didn't want to wait. "I wonder if we'll ever see him again? Do you think God might let us try to reach him once more? Maybe I should've said more. Would it have mattered, Marty?" he asked earnestly, his voice tight with longing.

"In the situation you were in, Shane, you couldn't really do much more than you did. I heard him say he had too many plans to fulfill. He said he didn't have time to die. What would you have said if you could have continued the conversation?"

Shane had only been saved for a month. He was progressing rapidly but hadn't had any experience in witnessing. He was willing to learn, though. "That's what I need to learn, Marty. I really don't know what I would have said next!"

Marty thought this would be a good time to continue his soul-winning lessons. "The best answer to his statement about not having time to die would be to remind him that coffins come in all sizes. Do you understand what I mean, Shane?"

"You mean death can come at any age? That's a good point. I want to learn more about witnessing, Marty. There are several people I need to talk to about Christ."

Erin was filled with gratitude as she watched Shane make the decisions she had prayed for with anxious hope. Her heart swelled as she silently thanked God, tears pricking her eyes. "Thank You, Lord. I love You so much," she prayed in quiet joy.

This Oregon summer night was remarkably calm. There wasn't even a breeze to keep the mosquitoes at bay. Riding with the top down was a pleasure only convertible owners could enjoy. It made starry nights seem more romantic. There was one drawback: whenever the wind-blown passengers arrived, they had to spend ten minutes putting their hair back in place, well, at least the long-haired girls did.

The '57 Chevy sped along Highway 99, pulling into the T&R Truck Stop. Mr. and Mrs. Lynch were already waiting for them. Mr. Lynch greeted Shane first, "I was really proud of the way you witnessed to that giant, Chris Nelson. If he can't scare you away, no one will ever do it. Keep up the good work, Shane. I'm sure God has some wonderful experiences in store for you."

When Erin was fixing her hair, she cornered Kosy

for another talk. Seeing Shane's progress made her hopeful about her own influence. "Kosy, isn't Shane doing well with his witnessing? He demonstrated a lot of courage—talking to that giant of a man! With more practice and information, he'll be very good at witnessing."

Kosy wasn't sure she was ready for that kind of experience. She worried about what others might think. "I don't think I could do what he did. It's too scary and embarrassing. What if someone laughs at me, Erin?"

"Kosy, you should never be ashamed to tell people about your salvation. Just think back on your experience of accepting Christ and share it with whoever God allows you to share it with. I can practice with you like Marty does with Shane. Are you willing to do that?" Kosy gave her a weak nod.

Later that evening, as they neared home, Shane needed to gas up. He pulled into the TP station, where Bowie stomped out to meet him, clearly upset. "What's eaten you, buddy?" Shane inquired.

Bowie's face darkened with anger as he filled the tank. "That jerk, Engelbert Farnsworth III, just left. Every time he comes by, he makes sure to put me down." With a furious thud, the big Native American kid pounded the gas pump, his frustration clearly visible in the night air.

Erin bristled with indignation and compassion for Bowie. She liked him—he was impossible not to like. Engelbert Farnsworth III, though, made her blood boil. "What does he say that hurts you so badly?" she asked, her voice low with empathy.

Bowie was watching the pump as he filled Shane's tank. "He calls me names, like chief, red man, and even 'injun.' He always treats me with disdain."

Marty was paying for Shane's gas. "Hey, Bowie, he treats everyone like that, even us white folks."

Kosy stepped out, nerves fluttering, and reached up to Bowie with genuine warmth. "We all like you, Bowie. You're a true friend. Do you want to come to church with us on Sunday? We could spend the whole day together—swimming in Crabtree Creek and just having fun," she offered, hopeful and kind.

"Sure," Erin piped in, "And you can eat lunch at our home. How about it, Bowie?"

"Well, we don't work on Sundays, but that's not because we're Christians. You know that we Nez Perce Indians are nature-spirit worshipers, don't you?"

"No, I really didn't know that," Kosy answered hopefully, "but that makes no difference to us. You're welcome at our church. Please say you'll come, Bowie."

The Nez Perce teenager appreciated these friends. "Okay, I'll come if my Dad allows me to. What time does it begin? Can I bring my twin sisters?" Shane nodded affirmatively. They'd be glad to have the whole family come if they wanted to. Bowie closed their conversation by explaining that his parents would be going to Eastern Oregon, and he had to babysit his sisters anyway.

Shane started the motor and shifted the four-on-the-floor into first gear. "We have Sunday School at 9:45 AM, and morning worship at 11:00. Come to both. You might find it quite different from what you had imagined."

As they pulled out and crossed the canal, Shane praised his sister, "Good job, Kosy. We'll have to add Bowie to our prayer list. If we're going to win him to Christ, we might have to find out some information about the Nez Perce religion."

Erin gave Kosy a wink and an approving smile. She wanted her to feel encouraged in witnessing. "See, Kosy, it wasn't that hard to begin witnessing, now was it?"

The youngest member of the gang started to explain herself, "That's witnessing? All I did was invite a friend to come to church. I don't see how that could be classified as witnessing."

Marty spoke first, "You're doing what's called friendship evangelism. It's making friends, working with a friend, or just being friendly. You get him to church, and then let Pastor Ballentine do the explaining. It's the most effective form of witnessing." Kosy was pleased to have started so successfully.

It was a short seven-mile drive from Lebanon to Brewster's Corner. Because of its higher prices, Shane never bought gas at the Brewster family's station, open since 1946. But today, he pulled up under the overhang of Brewster's tiny general store.

"Going to fill up again, Shane?" Erin asked, giggling.

"Right, Smarty, I only get one mile to the gallon. Just be patient. I'm going to get some protein." He hurried into the small store and returned with a few packs of sunflower seeds.

"Sunflower seeds?" Marty questioned. "What for, Shane? Do you have parrots at home?"

"Don't you Gringos know anything? Don't you ever read anything?" Shane was appalled. "Sunflower seeds are tasty. I eat them. It's the favorite snack of Clint Walker, and look how big and strong he is!"

Clint Walker was an American TV actor.

HEIGHT: 6' 6"
WEIGHT: 260 POUNDS

Suddenly, Shane changed directions. He went to the other side of the gas pump, kneeling where another car had been parked. Putting his finger to the ground, he pulled up something. He walked over closer to the light to examine it. He even smelled it. He did everything but put it on his tongue.

He came trotting over to the car, on the other side of the gas pumps, and blurted out excitedly, "At first, in the dark, I thought it was just differential fluid. But, look. It's blood!" He showed it to Marty.

"You're right, but what does it mean?"

"It means the car, which was parked right there, had something in the trunk that had recently been killed." Shane donned his investigation cap. "This blood is still fresh. It was even a little warm when I touched it. What kind of car was it?"

"It was a blue car, or was it black?" Erin pondered.

"No, not the color. The make of the car," Shane prodded.

Erin protested. "What do I look like, the latest issue of *Car and Driver* magazine?"

Shane started the '57 Chevy. "Can anyone at least tell me which way they went?"

All three pointed towards Lacomb. The Chevy threw a few pebbles and some dust into the air as Shane pulled out. He had a determined look on his face, wanting to stop the poachers to protect the deer population for himself and others. "I want to catch up with them. If these poachers aren't stopped, there won't be any deer left for us to hunt in the fall. How much of a head start did they get?"

"One minute," two out of three of them said in unison.

Shane noticed taillights about half a mile ahead, just going over the ridge. "Did any other cars pass since they pulled out?"

Erin was shaking her head. "As far as I can remember, no other cars passed us, right, Kosy?" Kosy nodded in agreement.

Marty strained his eyes, gazing down the dark road. "Yeah, I saw the taillights, too. Erin was right. No other car has passed this point. It must be them. Step on it, Shane. It's pedal-to-the-metal time."

Erin was excited and nervous at the same time. "If you must catch them, Shane, at least do it safely, okay? I want to see these poachers behind bars as much as you do. But, we don't want to see ourselves in the hospital, right?"

Kosy was not quite as anxious for action as the rest. She started nibbling on her fingernails. "What are we going to do if we can stop them? Certainly, we won't be able to arrest them, or even delay them."

"Don't worry, Little Sis," Shane tried to calm Kosy. "I'm not going to do anything stupid. And quit chewing your fingernails. I want to stop them, get their license number, and talk to them a little. Maybe I'll even get a chance to memorize their faces. I promise you, Kosy, there won't be any confrontation."

It was at times like this that Shane was glad he had a little extra power under the hood. When he hit forty miles per hour in second gear, he remembered what Sergeant Kochian had told him about the bored-out engine and the four-barrel carburetor.

By stomping down on the gas pedal, he engaged all

four barrels. The instant acceleration was frightening. It threw Marty and Kosy, who had been leaning forward, against the back seat. Erin's straw hat flew off into the ditch.

There was more to this motor than Sergeant Kochian had actually described. This was the first time Shane had punched it. The noise was deafening and a bit scary. This wasn't going to be a race. The other car had no reason to speed.

The road was straight, so there wasn't much danger. Shane was topping sixty miles per hour when he began to slow down because of the ridge. As he brought the nose of the car over the hump, he could see he had gained some ground on the supposed poachers.

Marty was getting nervous. His leg started to bounce on the floorboard. "Don't go any faster, Shane? We don't want the telephone poles looking like a picket fence."

"Just a bit further, Marty, and I'll be able to pull up beside them or get them to pull over." As Shane came closer, he started blinking his lights. Surprisingly, the other car pulled over to the side.

"This is too easy, Shane," Erin remarked with a skeptical tone. "I'm not liking this even one little bit."

When the driver got out of the car and began to walk indignantly back to the Chevy, Erin hid her face. She was peeking out between the fingers of one hand and twirling her pigtail with her other. "Oh no," she groaned. "Not him again."

6 - A Once in a Lifetime Deal

Engelbert Farnsworth III, already infamous, started his tirade, "Well, well, well, if it isn't little 'Shaney Boy' and his loyal followers. What's the big idea, Shane? Is there an emergency or something? Why were you signaling for me to stop?"

Shane was a bit embarrassed to say the least. "Uh ... I ... er ... I guess we got you mixed up with someone else."

"Well, I've never been anyone else. I've always been myself, good old Engelbert Farnsworth III. Your girlfriend, whatever her name is, OUGHT to hide behind her hands. I'd be ashamed to be seen with this bunch of knuckleheads, too."

Shane was still stammering, "All ... all ... I can say is: We're sorry."

"You're right about that. This is the sorriest group I've ever encountered. But I'll give you credit for one thing. What you lack in smarts, you make up for in ignorance."

"Come on, Bert, leave the kids alone," someone yelled

from the Ford.

"Okay, Linda, but let me say goodbye to my friends first. See you guys on the first day of school. This year will be hilarious with Lacomb's THREE STOOGES on campus."

As Bert drove away, the gang finally relaxed. Shane pulled Erin's hand away from her face. "You can come out now. The boogie man is gone," he joked.

"That was very embarrassing, Shane," she complained vigorously. "What happened?"

Shane looked bewildered. "The only thing I can figure is that the poachers pulled off onto a side road, and then our buddy here pulled his car onto the main road. Rats, we lost them. Is there anything else that could go wrong? MURPHY STRIKES AGAIN."

Marty wasn't happy at the turn of events either. "Why does MURPHY always have to show up as an uninvited guest wherever we go?"

"Let's put our heads together before we lose our train of thought," Shane suggested to the others. "Was there anything unusual about that car which would help us identify it, anything at all, besides the fact it was blue or black?"

"Shane, I noticed something strange about it," Kosy added. "It had a front grill that looked like chicken wire. Does that help?"

"Help? Kosy, you just described a Studebaker. Was it

short and narrow?"

Marty added, "No, it was long and wide, I'm sure of that. It had whitewall tires."

"Then it's a Nash, a blue or black Nash." Shane's familiarity with cars proved helpful again. The Lacomb detectives had a lively discussion the rest of the way home. They were trying to figure out how they could put an end to the poaching.

As they passed Gentry's Hill, Shane noticed a lit-up FOR SALE sign on the side of a 1954 Chevrolet Bel Air. "Aren't you looking for a car, Marty? Maybe we can come by tomorrow and ask about that one. The '54 Chevys were really well made."

"A '54 Chevy! Shane, do you realize that car is only eight years old? Dad is only allowing me $100 to buy a car. No way could I buy a 1954 Chevy for that amount. About the only car I'm going to get for that price will have a crank on the front. You'll have to push it to start it, or always park it on a hill."

Shane was waiting for an opportunity like this. "Oh, ye of little faith. If it's God's will, you'll get it for that price, right?" Shane almost surprised himself. He raised his eyebrows and added, "Did I just say that? I must be quoting Pastor Ballentine. I certainly didn't make that idea up myself."

It was true. He said it, and all the kids heard him. This was a giant leap for a new Christian. He had come a long distance in a short period of time. It takes some new believers decades to start tithing and trusting like Shane did, even after only a month as a Christian.

"Right," Marty was hearing his first sermon from this new Christian. "Okay, preacher, come by tomorrow before lunch, and we'll see what God can do with one hundred dollars."

School was getting closer, and Marty needed a car. Mr. Lynch thought he was being very generous with his son. Marty thought so, too, and he wasn't the type to forget it, either.

As Shane pulled into the yard, Mr. Lynch was still conversing with his son. "I can only give you that much, Marty. The extra insurance will cost me an additional $30 each month. So, you and Shane had better look really hard and pray a lot."

Marty climbed into Shane's car. "Well, I only have this one hundred dollars to buy that 1954 Chevy. What do you think he'll ask for the car?"

"Nuts," Shane answered discouragingly, "if it runs

well, he should ask at least five hundred dollars. What are we going to do?"

"Yesterday you were preaching at me, and now you're asking me? I plan to do the only thing that'll bring about the results you preached about yesterday—PRAY. One of my favorite verses is Jeremiah 33:3, '*Call upon Me and I will answer thee, and show thee great and mighty things which thou knowest not.*' That's a good promise, isn't it?"

These were the promises Shane needed. "Where did you say that verse was? That's one I need to memorize. I'm not very comfortable praying out loud yet, so you go ahead."

Marty bowed his head. "God, You know I want a car. I'll promise to drive responsibly and be thankful. Please help me get this car, if it's Your will. In Jesus' name, Amen."

Shane was impressed by Marty's short, sincere prayer. "Here we go." They both carefully inspected the '54 Chevy as they pulled into the yard.

"Hey, you guys. Come to see the car? Alright! My name is Justin Kase. My mom has been after me to get this car off the front lawn," he pointed to the cream-colored Chevy. "I bought a new car, so I really need to get rid of this eyesore. What'll you give me for it?"

Marty blurted out, "I've got a ..."

"Look at the car first," Shane finished his sentence as he nudged him on the shoulder.

Justin looked a bit concerned. "Well, the battery's dead. When I tried to start it by pushing, it wouldn't take off. As you can see, there's one bald tire on the front. The other three are only so-so."

Shane was curious, "Can we try pulling it, Justin? By the way, is that your real name, or are you pulling our leg?"

"Weird, isn't it? I'm telling you the truth. My real name is Justin Kase. I've always had to explain it to people who were paying attention. Some kids grow up to hate their parents when they do this to them. Man, I knew a girl whose last name was Christmas, and her mother named her Mary. That's TOO MUCH aggravation. And sure, we can pull the car. I even have a rope here you can use."

Shane tied the '54 Chevy to his car. Marty got behind the wheel of the Bel Air. Shane gave him some vital last-minute instructions. "Put it in second, and when we hit fifteen miles per hour, pop the clutch. Be sure the key is on."

Each time Marty popped the clutch, the back wheels just froze, throwing rocks and plowing gravel. After three tries with the same result, Justin drove up. "See what I mean. If it won't start, how can I sell it to anyone?"

"How much do you want for it, as is?" Marty asked hopefully.

"Seventy-five dollars."

"Twenty-five," Shane offered rapidly.

"Fifty, and not a penny less," Justin insisted.

"Thirty-five, and that's our final offer," Shane insisted.

Marty was in shock, too dumbfounded to even whisper a word.

"Okay, it's yours," the reluctant seller gave in. "Cash on the barrel head, or no deal." Marty peeled off the money, and Justin signed the title. "See you around. I hope you can get it going."

Shane waited until the seller got out of sight, then he began to do a victory dance around the car. "SOLD TO THE AMERICAN TEENAGER! WOW, WHAT A DEAL WE MADE!"

Marty was still scratching his head, "Are you sure we made a good deal? It doesn't have air conditioning, you know!"

"Sure it does. Just let me show you how to turn it on." With that, the Woods kid opened the door and rolled down the window. Marty just had to laugh. Shane was so funny.

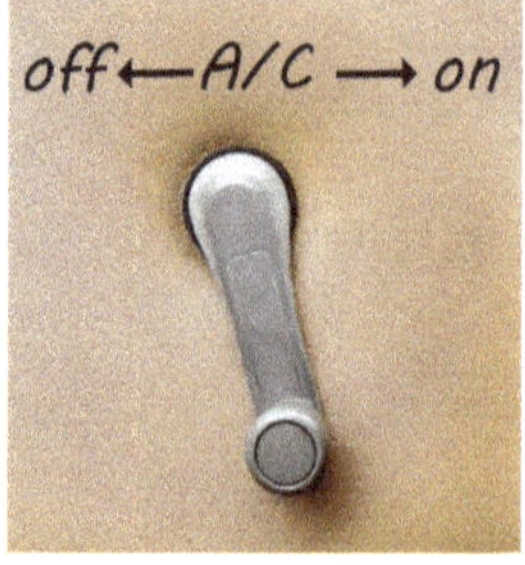

"Marty, you just made the buy of the century!" Shane raised his eyebrows. "Even if we have to replace the transmission or the whole motor, you made a terrific deal. You could pull it to the junk yard and they'd give you $300 just for the parts. I'm sure of it.

"Now let's take a closer look at the motor and try to find out what's wrong. It must be something fairly simple. Justin didn't have the patience or knowledge to work the problem out."

Marty lifted the hood. "What do you expect to find? Will we really have to exchange the motor? Can we pull it home?"

"Why so many questions? Let me check a few things. It's definitely locking the wheels. But why?"

Shane poked around the motor area. "Put it in neutral." Marty tried, but it remained stuck. "Try shifting into any gear." There was still no response. Shane put his hand on the shifting gears of the steering column. "Try shifting it again." This time, Shane helped him.

"Aha, just as I thought. It was locked in reverse. That's why it wouldn't start and just threw rocks all over the road. Let me move a few of these gears, PRONTO! Now shift it into second. Let's try it again."

"Will it start with a dead battery?" Marty asked.

"Sure, it will. I think we solved the problem." Shane pulled the Chevy again. When Marty reached the right speed, he popped the clutch. The Bel Air motor sprung to life. Marty was so exuberant he started pounding his fist on the steering wheel and squealing with joy.

When they drove into the Rocking L Ranch, Mr. Lynch couldn't believe his eyes. "How could you buy that car with only one hundred dollars?"

"I didn't," Marty squealed with laughter, "I bought it for only thirty-five dollars." Now, it was Marty's turn to do his victory dance around the car. "God answered my prayer, and now I even have enough money left to buy a new battery and some tires. Thanks for getting me such a great deal. I'm going to start calling you Thrifty Scotsman."

"That was the fastest and most direct answer to the shortest and most sincere prayer I've ever witnessed," Shane said as he gave Marty a friendly slap on the back. "I can't wait until we drive into town and show Bowie. He'll go nuts. This has to be the best deal since Steward bought Alaska from the Russians."

Driving the '54 Chevy to town was a joy ride for two teens. It only had 56,000 miles on it. The body was rust-free. To buy a car that was only eight years old for thirty-five dollars was unthinkable. IT WAS THE PURCHASE OF THE CENTURY!

Marty remembered his promise to God to be responsible and thankful. He knew that would take determination. It's so easy to be irresponsible and unthankful. Marty was raised in a Christian home, a definite advantage the Woods kids didn't have. He knew what his task was. He'd been taught "to whom much is given, much is required." He planned on doing his part. He was thankful.

They pulled into Bud's Shell Service on Park and Grant. Marty asked Bud the price of a new tire and battery. "A new tire will run about fifteen dollars. I have a used battery you can have for five dollars. Will that put you in business?"

"You bet, Mr. Grant," Marty answered. "In fact, we'll take four new tires. I can use the so-so tire on the front as the spare. Wow, that's exactly one hundred dollars. Thirty-five for the car, tires ($60), and battery ($5). God has been good to me, and I'm not going to forget it."

Gratitude was a way of life for a Christian who remembered and cared about what Christ had done for him. This is the attitude Marty wanted to have in his life, and it's the message he wanted to share with the world. An ATTITUDE OF GRATITUDE was the theme he needed in his teen years.

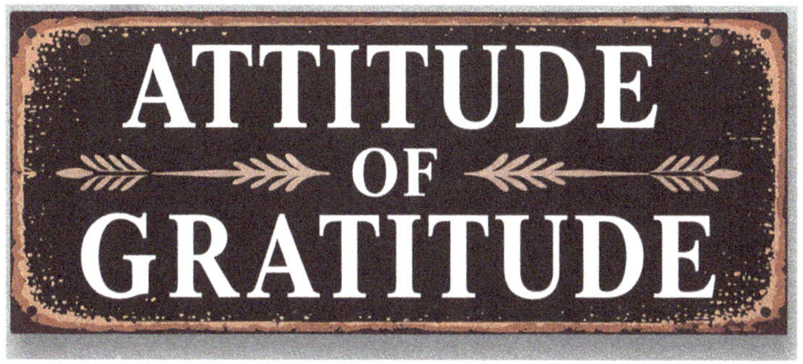

"What was that you said, Sonny?" Mr. Grant asked as he cocked his head in Marty's direction.

"Nothing. I was talking to Shane."

After changing the tires, they drove to the T.P. Oil Company. "Too bad Bowie's dad doesn't sell these extras," Marty remarked. "I could've bought them here."

Bowie was topping off a tank and receiving the money. "Thank you, Mrs. Ellsworth. Do you want me to check your oil?" Bowie meandered over to his friends, who were leaning against a Chevy. They were grinning from ear to ear. "You guys look like the cats that just swallowed the mice. What's up?"

Both boys looked into the sky, squinting their eyes, with their hands above their eyebrows to see what was "UP."

"Okay, clowns, I deserve that. Now tell me where you got this car?" Bowie pounded the hood with his fist and kicked a tire. Marty told him about Shane's new nickname.

Shane filled him in on the deal. "Wow, I need the Thrifty Scotsman to buy a car for me," Bowie slapped Shane on the back. "Congratulations! My dad said I could get a car if it weren't too expensive. By the way, how did you do at the tournament last weekend, Marty? I wanted to go, but I had to practice for the upcoming rodeo."

"I didn't do as well as I wanted, but I enjoyed the experience, though. When will we go to the rodeo?"

Bowie appreciated Marty's interest. "I was just at Joseph in Eastern Oregon for Chief Joseph Days. I took second place in bull riding and first in calf roping. The next event is a warm-up rodeo, preparing everyone for the big one in September— the Pendleton Roundup. I'm counting on you guys coming over to Eastern Oregon to root for me. You're coming, aren't you?"

"We sure are," they both promised in unison. Their affirmative answer pleased Bowie. They also wanted to know if Bowie was going to take his twin sisters. He said they couldn't go because his parents wanted them to help paint the house.

A pickup pulled into the station. Bowie signaled for them to accompany him to the customer. "I'd like to introduce you guys to a friend of mine. Mike Whitesell, these are my good friends, Marty Lynch and Shane Woods. Mike works as an announcer at KGAL, you know, Lebanon's radio station outside of town."

Shane looked like a bulb just lit up in his head. He started stroking his chin. "Hey, I've got a great idea that might catch some of those no-good poachers. Mr. Whitesell, can you give community announcements on the radio?"

"What did you have in mind, Shane?"

"Well, we've been trying to catch some poachers. They keep slipping out of our hands. All we have on them is their car. It's a 1950 Nash. You know, the one with the wire-meshed front grill. We also know it has whitewall tires. If you could give an announcement that someone REALLY wants to buy a 1950 Nash, maybe we could get them to take the bait." Shane blinked his eyes and smirked. "Will you help us catch them?"

"Okay, it is a deal," Mike promised with a handshake. "When do you want to set them up? What are you going to do if they show? Will it be a citizen's arrest? That could be dangerous."

"No, not exactly," Shane bowed out, "I'll have Sergeant Kochian hiding around the corner with a search warrant in his hand. How about tomorrow afternoon for the announcement? The meeting could be scheduled for three o'clock in the high school parking lot."

"Fine. You're on, kid. I also hate poachers."

Bowie approached Shane rather excitedly. "Really, Shane, do you actually think we can buy that Nash for three hundred dollars? Dad said I could get a car for that much."

"Are you serious, Bowie?" Marty asked.

"Yes, I'm serious. I need a car, and this sounds like an excellent opportunity to get one cheaply. I bet those robbers will be looking to dump theirs. Will you make the deal for me, Thrifty Scotsman? I think that's what you had in mind, right?"

Shane didn't know if he liked this new title. At least it was not self-proclaimed. He didn't know whether he was being complimented or teased. That was yet to be learned. "You win, Bowie. I'll do my best. That's kind of what I had in mind."

"One last suggestion," Bowie explained, "wait until he signs the title before you sic Sergeant Kochian on him."

Mike Whitesell sounded very convincing on the KGAL Community Line. Someone was REALLY looking for a 1950 Nash. Bowie, Marty, and Shane waited at the high school parking lot. Marty looked worried, "Do you think they'll be armed?"

"I doubt it," Shane tried to sound confident. "There may only be one. I can't imagine a shoot-out. Look, here comes a Nash into the lot. Now, Marty, don't give us away with your nervous leg!"

"But, it's white," Marty noted with a smirk.

"And there come two more Nash cars from the other direction, a black one and a blue one," Bowie announced nervously. "What ... what are we going to do now?"

Shane took charge. "Bowie, you take the white one and stall. Look interested, but don't make any promises. Marty, you take the black one and I'll do the same with the blue one. Now separate to the corners of the lot, and wave your car over to your corner."

"Quit looking so nervous, you guys," Shane ordered. "This is even better. We'll definitely get a lower price. Marty, whichever car has whitewall tires is the poacher. I'll trade with you if your car is the poacher."

After an initial introduction, the three met for a pow-wow. "The white one is a real beauty," Bowie shook his head. "It has an all-wood dashboard. Unfortunately, he wants one thousand dollars for it."

"How about the black one, Marty? It looks like you got the poacher, since it's the only car with whitewalls. I'll trade with you as we planned," Shane suggested as he turned and headed for the black Nash.

Marty was relieved. He didn't relish confronting crooks face-to-face. It was much harder than witnessing. "He wants five hundred dollars. You can have him," he shouted after Shane.

Shane approached the suspected poacher. "I'm representing the buyer. He'll give you two hundred dollars today, cash on the old barrel head."

"Is this some joke, kid? Are you really planning on buying my car?" the burly man asked. He was not a

pleasant person, definitely not someone you would invite to Thanksgiving dinner. He could be capable of carving up other things besides the turkey.

"That's our offer, take it or leave it," Shane tried to sound like the Thrifty Scotsman, living up to his new reputation. His voice was firm, betraying nothing of the nervous flutter beneath his calm exterior.

The trio parleyed again. "How's our used-car buyer doing?" Bowie wanted to know. "What's the price now?"

"He said he would take three hundred fifty dollars for it and throw in two mounted buck horns. I'll bet they're fresh, too. I'll try to get him down more, but he's getting abusive. I'll be right back."

Shane approached the belligerent seller. "We'll give you three hundred dollars, and not a penny more, if you have the title here and sign it today. Oh, don't worry about a ride home. We already have that arranged!"

Shane waved Bowie over to the black Nash. Marty was clapping his hands as he yelled, "Sold to the Nez Perce teen. Now you can give your sisters a ride to school and to the grocery store, right?"

After the money was exchanged for a signed title, Shane waved Sergeant Kochian in from around the corner. When Old Sourpuss saw the patrol car coming, he got antsy. "Hey, what's going on here?" He lit out across the grass, heading for the baseball diamond.

Bowie was the first to move. It was a short foot race with the Nez Perce tackling the bad paleface at both knees. Shane was right behind him. "Good takedown, Bowie, two points Nez Perce, zero poacher. You win, Bowie, if you don't let him escape. Sit on his face."

"Nice tackle, Bowie," Sergeant Kochian bragged. "Are you going out for football this fall? The Warriors could use you on their first-year team. I'm the assistant coach."

Upon a quick search of the trunk, Sergeant Kochian found deer hair and traces of fresh blood. There was enough evidence to put the scoundrel in the poky for a while. His name was Tra Bull. He wasn't giving out 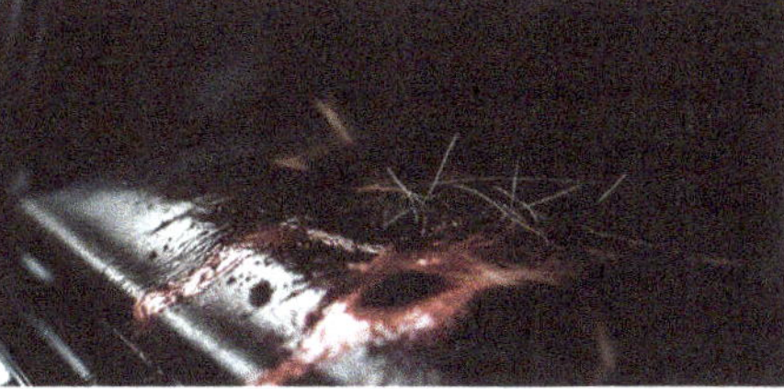 any information about his cohorts.

Since the crook didn't need the money because the state would cover his living expenses, Sergeant Kochian returned the $300 to Bowie. "You just earned yourself a used car. I'll fill out the paperwork to transfer it to your dad's name, if he agrees. You should be able to pick it up from the impound lot tomorrow, after we take pictures and get all the evidence we'll need in case we have to go to trial. However, I'm sure the prosecutor will offer Mr. Bull a sweet plea deal to give up the names of his buddies in exchange for his own freedom."

As promised, the next day, the police completed their investigation, the prosecutor obtained a confession (and the names of the poaching crew members), and the judge ordered the release of the seized car. Bowie picked up the car and used the money Sergeant Kochian had returned to pay his insurance premium to Bilyeu's Insurance Company.

7 - Frogman Training

Julia was baking a chocolate cake when Shane and Kosy walked through the door. Their grandma, known for her excellent cooking, often filled the Woods's kitchen with enticing smells, especially on holidays like Thanksgiving and Christmas. Shane remembered these moments fondly.

Sunday meals stood out the most. Grandma always made pot roast or fried chicken with mashed potatoes, brown gravy, and a fruit pie. This delicious food was the way to a teen's heart.

Grandpa Woods was coming in the door with a large bucket of milk. As he was filtering it, he addressed the two of them, "We got a letter from Thomas today. If you want, I'll read it to all of us!"

Kosy put down her purse and hugged both of her grandparents. "Sure, we'd love to hear it. We've been praying for Thomas."

~~~~~~

To My Dear Family,

I want to thank Grandma for her care package. She knows how much I love her chocolate chip cookies. We owe both Grandpa and Grandma a great deal, more than we could ever repay. Many times, they've bailed us out of trouble by taking us into their hearts and home.

All three of us love you dearly and certainly want you to know it. We'd really be in trouble if you hadn't taken Shane and Kosy into your hearts again. So, here I am on Coronado Island in the San Diego Bay, at the Underwater Demolition Team, or "Frogman" School. Perhaps you should know a little more about what I'll be doing.

But first, the weather here is just fantastic. Each day it gets up to about eighty degrees and down to sixty at night. The sunsets are colorful and would make great photos if I had a camera. I certainly will enjoy that part of my stay here.

Our job will be to find and clear obstacles from assault beaches so amphibious crafts can land there, with troops and equipment. Right now, you're probably asking yourself, "What obstacles?" The enemy uses various obstacles to protect shorelines from invasion: steel and concrete girders, logs, barbed wire, and sharp stakes (as well as mines). Then there are natural obstacles such as sandbars, rock formations, and coral reefs.

Our training period is twenty-one weeks. Usually, less than one-third of the sailors make it to the last week. Our first three weeks have been spent getting into shape, that is, taking all those waffles
~~~~~~

and strawberry shortcake off the waistline!

We had many long, forced marches and a five-mile run every day. There are several obstacle courses we have to complete in a limited time.

The next seven days is called "ELIMINATION WEEK," because so many have dropped out during that time. So far, I'm doing fine. I'm not looking forward to next week, but I'll pass. I'm determined not to quit.

I've also met another frogman named Richard Edwards. He's from Quincy, Illinois, and is a really nice guy. He invited me to go to the Baptist Church with him on Wednesday night. I think I'll go. Pray for me, I really feel the need for it.

Love,
Thomas

~~~~~~

"I wish Thomas could've been here all summer. He could've gone to the Timber Carnival with us," Kosy lamented. "He could help us catch these rotten poachers, too. I'm going to write him and tell him how I got saved. Maybe that'll help him understand what it's all about."

Kosette took her time before accepting Christ. She struggled to understand how God could love her while allowing mistreatment from her mother. Pastor Ballentine gave her the best explanation she had heard.

He explained that God didn't create robots but gave everyone free will to choose good or evil. Many people
~~~~~~

choose to do good, but good works don't save anyone. Some choose to do wrong, which causes others—especially family members—to suffer greatly.

"Good idea, Kosy," Shane encouraged his sister. "Yeah, Thomas is always a big help. I'm sure he'd enjoy putting these no-good crooks in the slammer. We've only got one so far. There must be a few more of them out there. If we can't stop them, there won't be any fawns left for next year's hunting season."

"Today, I have a hankering to go swimming in The Channels at the Snow Peak Bridge. Let's call Marty and Erin to see if they'll meet us there in one hour. Grandpa, will you help me finish wiring the jeep to get it ready?"

Grandpa put his arm around Shane's shoulder as they walked to the garage. "I can hardly believe how much the Lord has changed you, Shane. Since you accepted Christ as your Savior, you're a completely different person. God certainly has blessed you. Don't forget His grace and kindness to you."

"I'm still quite young in the Lord, Grandpa. I want to learn more. I have no idea where Mom is. Wouldn't it be nice if she came to know Christ, too? As far as remembering what Christ did for me and what God is doing for me now, I'll never forget. If you think I need to be reminded, feel free to give me a jolt or two."

"Are you praying, Shane?" Grandpa asked.

"Yes, I am, and expecting God to answer me, according to His will, of course. I have lots to pray for. I hope someday Bowie will abandon his Spiritism beliefs and come to Christ."

Grandpa knew the next thing he was going to say would be hard to swallow. "I know it sounds strange, but you could even pray for Engelbert Farnsworth III. He certainly needs to be saved. I know he's a difficult person to like, and nothing but a thorn in your flesh. You might see things turn around someday, and prayer will be the instrument that'll bring it to pass."

"That's going to be difficult," Shane confessed. "I'm not sure I'm up to that."

"That's what Christ said: 'Pray for them which despitefully use you, and persecute you.' If we believe John 3:16, then we must believe the rest of the Bible which includes this idea in Matthew 5:44. It won't be easy. Be sure you don't give him any fuel for his persecution fire. I'll also pray. Now, what do we lack to get this jeep on the road?"

Shane was thankful for Grandpa's many years of experience in engine mechanics. He could fix almost anything, including diesel engines. He never had to pay for a repair job. "I think the timing is still a little off, Grandpa."

Grandpa lifted the small hood. "Get in, Shane, and turn the motor over." When the engine started rotating, flames roared up near the carburetor. "Stop, Shane, turn it off," Grandpa yelled over the noise of the engine.

"You were right, it does need some more work on the timing."

After a few minor adjustments, the four-cylinder engine was running like a top. Grandpa slapped Shane on the back, "You have a real good machine here, Sonny. All we had to do was change the wiring and clean up the inside of the motor. We can use this jeep to hunt deer. Now off you go, and have a good time."

Summer was fading away. Soon fall signs would be everywhere. Then in the early morning, Shane would actually be able to see his breath. Also, each leaf that turned a bright color was only a promise that soon the whole tree would follow suit.

The maple trees, in all their breathtaking array of colors, would make the evergreens look dull. But, in the dead of winter, the green branches, reaching skyward, would mock the empty, barren ones.

Shane was preparing for the last hurrah in the clear waters of The Snow Peak Channels before school started. The water was already cool enough to require a gingerly entrance. Splashing someone on the back demanded a hearty reprisal.

Marty was on his knees, drinking from a clear, quiet pool, watching the crayfish chase the minnows. Shane pushed his head under the water. "Better drink a lot now, Marty. When the rains start, this river is going to be so muddy the trout are going to have to use road maps, or should I say river maps?"

With no time for courtesy, water fights became the

day's activity. The minnows scattered, and Kosy joined Marty in getting even with Shane. Suddenly, Kosy raised her hand to get everyone's attention. "Is that thunder, or am I imagining things?" she asked.

Erin cupped her ears. "I don't hear anything, besides the sky is clear." She continued splashing Kosy and Marty. She had taken Shane's side.

After plenty of dunking and fun, Shane searched for red devil spinners but found nothing. Kosy made a face. "Look, Shane, why are all these dead fish floating by us? Yuck, I'm getting out of the water."

Shane scanned the water. "All these fish are smaller than six inches—the legal limit," he commented.

"And there's that thunder again," Kosy convinced the rest. "But, I still don't see any clouds."

Shane cocked his head and cupped his ears. "That definitely isn't thunder. Someone is dynamiting Digangi's Lake, about one mile upstream. That's why these small fish are floating dead downstream. Let's take a look. It's probably the same poachers."

"Shane, if they have dynamite, that could be really dangerous," Marty warned.

"We won't try to arrest them," Shane promised. "We'll just see who they are. I promise we'll stay out of sight."

The jeep pulled out with four curious but nervous teens, eager to put an end to the disgraceful poaching in their area. The trail to Digangi's Lake was off the paved road. It was only wide enough for one vehicle. The small saplings kept brushing against the jeep's roll bar.

Every so often, a couple of chipmunks would tear across the trail. Chip and Dale didn't make it all the way across, but they were smart enough to pause under the jeep as it passed over. Saved by their instincts.

There was one more thunderous explosion as the jeep topped the hill. Shane pulled off the trail, hiding behind a fallen giant Douglas Fir. He pointed the jeep downhill and left it in second gear, with the key on. He didn't want to be unprepared.

Marty jumped out and looked through his binoculars. "There's a small boat in the lake. All I can make out are two men. Wait a minute, there's another gent on the shore."

Shane was getting nervous. He was scratching his head and could feel his stomach tightening up like a rubber band on a balsa wood plane. "Can you recognize any of them, or can't you see their faces clearly?"

"I can't see them very well from this distance. Maybe we could sneak a bit closer." Marty started to advance. "Kosy and Erin can stay here."

"Now look at who's getting brave or foolish. I thought Shane said we were going to maintain our distance. This is NOT maintaining our distance," Erin told Kosy.

The duo crouched down and weaved their way through the trees and bushes until they were close to the water's edge. "We've got to make sure we have enough time to get away, if we're discovered," Shane planned. "I wish I'd left the jeep running. Hindsight is easier than foresight."

Marty was adjusting the binoculars. "This is a lot better. I can make out their faces clearly now."

"Do you know any of them? How about the guy on the shore?"

Marty handed the glasses to Shane. "I've never seen any of them before. How about you? Take a look."

Shane peered through the spy glasses. "The guys in the boat, I don't know. That toothless dude on the shore sure looks familiar."

They both gawked at each other, and Marty blurted out, "The drunk who climbed up the electric pole. Remember, we took him home that night? It's him again, I'm sure of it. He knocked all of his teeth out when he put his wet cigarette on the power line."

"Why, of course," Shane muttered disgustedly, "how stupid of me! Remember, when we took him home, I spotted blood on their car? They have to be part of the group that's poaching, although there may be more involved."

"They only live a few miles from us. I think they're renting the old Simon place," Marty surmised.

Shane looked through the glasses again. "I see an ugly car by the lake. It looks like a homemade job. It must be their only vehicle. We'll have to notify Sergeant Kochian. He can search their place. Wait a minute! There seems to be some excitement on the boat. They're shouting and pointing this way."

"They must've spotted us by some reflection off the binocular lens, Shane," Marty guessed. "We'd better make tracks."

The toothless guy on the shore picked up his shotgun and let fly both barrels. Fortunately, he was out of range. His pellets fell harmlessly into the lake, far short of the boys.

"We might not be so lucky next time. He could use a lead slug." Shane took off for the jeep with Marty in hot pursuit. "Hurry up, Marty, we've got to get out of here."

Marty shouted, "Erin, start the jeep."

"Does she know how?" the owner worried.

"I hope so."

Erin motioned for Kosy to get in the jeep. She turned the motor over, and it caught hold. Unfortunately, she didn't know Shane had left it in second gear. The Willys Jeep jolted forward. Erin was steering downhill, whether she liked it or not. This was not what the girls had in mind when they decided to keep at a safe distance and just have a look-see.

Shane and Marty were 'good griefing' it halfway down the hill. "Keep it on the road, Erin. Step on the brakes a little," Shane yelled as best as he could.

Because she slowed the jeep, Shane was able to catch up. He grabbed the roll bar and swung aboard. "Scoot over, girl, I'm taking charge." With that, she slid over to the co-pilot's seat, and Shane plopped his hide in the driver's place and took the steering wheel.

Marty took hold of the other roll bar and swung into the back seat. "Pedal to the metal, Shane. Old Toothless is topping the ridge. He's aiming that cannon right …"

A thunderous clap cut off Marty's words. Fortunately, that's all it cut off. The twelve-gauge slug whizzed over their heads. "This is too close for comfort," Shane complained as they hit Snow Peak Road and headed for home.

They knew a chewing out would be the order of the day when Sergeant Kochian heard the story of this narrow escape. He didn't want them this close to any flying bullets. It wasn't necessary and certainly not good for their health. 'I told you so' would be the menu for the visit to the police station.

Richard Edwards was a weatherman on our radar picket ship. He befriended me and invited me to church. He retired from the Navy and has been a pastor for 40 years. His church supported us in our missionary work. A better friend a sailor never had.

8 - The Eastern Trip

Engelbert Farnsworth III routinely caused trouble for Linn County law enforcement. He didn't respect rules and bullied others at school. Shane and his friends already knew this. The game warden wanted to catch him poaching, but Bert always managed to avoid getting caught.

John Yelle, one of the game wardens, spotted Bert fishing in Crabtree Creek, using waders up to his armpits. "Do you have a fishing license, Bert?" John was sure he didn't.

Bert was a smart mouth, "Sure, I do. Yes, Sirrrrre, I certainly do."

John was confident Bert was lying, so he asked him to bring over his license. Bert refused and said, "If you want to see it, you'll have to wade out here. I'm busy trying to catch rainbow trout."

That was all the encouragement John needed. He carefully waded into the creek. When asked for the license, Bert handed it over with a smug smile. John, now soaked, realized Bert had outsmarted him again.

John went back to the office to change clothes and was soon called by Sergeant Kochian for help with some junior detectives.

Everyone in Sergeant Kochian's office felt tense. The officer was clearly upset. "You kids are taking big risks. You HAVE to be more careful. These are dangerous people, not the kind who sit quietly in church. I don't want anyone getting hurt. Understand?"

"We didn't think they'd see us," Shane tried to defend himself and calm the nervous sergeant at the same time. "They must've seen a reflection from the binocular lens."

The sergeant continued, "I'm serious, kids. I care about all of you and don't want to see anyone hurt. I went to their rented farm, but they'd already left and didn't leave a forwarding address."

At that point, the sergeant called in the game warden. "Meet John Yelle, one of Linn County's three game wardens. He has some advice for you."

John started, "I agree with the sergeant. These people are dangerous. Don't take risks. I'll give you my phone number. Call me if you see anything unusual."

"Looks like we're back to zero," Marty complained. Noticing Sergeant Kochian's look, he thought he should change his story. Guessing what he might say next, Marty added, "I mean YOU TWO are back to ZERO, Sir."

Shane liked Sergeant Kochian but was not intimidated by his personality, unlike Marty, who seemed to be. "Don't worry about us, Sergeant, we're all in the hands of God, and we're careful. Sometimes it just seems we're in the right place at the right time."

Kosy remembered what Shane had said previously. "Is it in the wrong place at the right time or in the right place at the wrong time? Now you're saying we're in the right place at the right time. Confusionville, Oregon, that's where I live."

"You guys take it easy," Sergeant Kochian ordered, "and try to inform me before you go playing 'Cops & Robbers' or 'Dick Tracy.' Okay?"

"We'll do our best," Erin replied for all four. "But we don't have walkie-talkies or CB radios, Sergeant."

"Hey, if things get any hotter around here, I think I'll have a police radio installed in a '57 Chevy at the city's expense. Now get out of here, you guys, and be good," were the sergeant's last words.

Pulling into the T.P. Oil Company was a ritual all four anticipated. Bowie always had a smile and a kind word, but this time he verbalized his discontent. "So, I miss out on all the fun and games of Lebanon's only teenage detective agency. That's not fair. I guess I'll have to stir up some of my own excitement. Are you guys going to the rodeo with me this weekend?"

"We're planning on it, Bowie," Shane spoke up first. "When do you want us to meet you here?"

"It won't be easy," he warned them. "It's a six-hour drive. We'd better leave tomorrow. That way, we'll have time to rest the horses and, of course, we'll need some rest too. I don't want to punish my new Nash, so I'll use my dad's pickup to pull the horse trailer. You guys can follow me. I'll arrange sleeping quarters for you with some of my fine relatives."

"And just exactly WHERE will we sleep, Bowie?" Kosy asked with a funny look on her face, hoping she hadn't offended her Native American friend.

"My dear Little White Princess, I can guarantee it won't be in a tepee or a wigwam," Bowie tried to humor Kosy. "I have some well-to-do relatives who raise Herefords at a place called Sweet P Ranch. What do you say we meet here at noon tomorrow? You'll really enjoy the experience. I'll make you a promise. If, when we get back, you've not had a good trip, you don't have to go!"

Shane wasn't falling for that. "Alright, Bowie, we'll go; but no more of your forked-tongue double talk, savvy?"

Back at the farm, Grandma agreed to let them go. "You all need one more adventure before school starts."

"Thanks, Grandma," Kosy said. "At least this year we don't have to buy our school clothes at Polly Potter's Used Clothing Trailer." This was one of Kosy's concerns that was resolved by using the $1,000 she got from the reward money.

Suddenly, the phone rang with the Wood's party-line signal—two long rings and a short. "I'll get it for you, Grandma,"

Kosy ran for the phone, tripped on the rug, slid to the bureau, and picked up the receiver. At the same time, Shane held his arms straight out to each side like a baseball umpire and called, "Safe! You're safe at home, Kosy." Sometimes, Kosy thought her brother was a little crazy!

Erin spoke lowly to Kosy on the phone. "It's too bad we don't have another person going. If we did, you could sit in the front with Shane and me." Erin was being a bit manipulative, for a good personal reason!

"Why would I want to sit in the middle? I like window seats."

"No, silly, I'll sit in the middle, and even closer to Shane because you'll be by the window." Sometimes Erin thought Kosy was naive, or was she?

"I could always ask Shane's old friend, Linda McCarn, to come along," Kosy teased.

She wasn't as naive as Erin thought. "No way, Jose. We'll keep it just as it is," Erin quit while she was ahead.

When Shane and company pulled into Bowie's gas station, the sun was already high in the sky, leaving short shadows on the ground. Bowie laid the map out on the counter. "We'll start out going east, hit the freeway at Albany, and go north on Highway 99, bypassing Portland and catching the Hood River Highway. Then, it's right on to Pendleton. You should follow me, so we can go at my speed, understand?"

The group left at noon, heading east. Shane, used his tour guide voice: "To the right is Cent-Wise Drug Store. Last chance for Butterfingers or Snickers for the next 150 miles!"

"That's a lie," Marty blurted out. "I brought two in my back pocket. Oops, it's Butterfingers crumbs now."

The ride to Albany was uneventful. The freeway north was great. Driving through Salem, they could see the

courthouse with its bright dome and the famous Golden Pioneer standing tall.

Most of the land around the capital was used for fruit and vegetable farming. In Salem, there were many canning factories. This was the peak season for green beans and mint. "Maybe some day ..." Shane projected, "maybe some day, we'll come up here and visit the State Fair." That got a majority yell.

There was a stop in Milwaukee for hot dogs and Cokes. Shane checked the oil in both vehicles. He made sure the hood on Bowie's pickup was latched down tight. "Ready to roll." Skirting around Portland to avoid traffic, the slow-moving caravan turned east along the Columbia River.

This part of the drive was scenic. Tall cliffs rose on the right, while the Columbia River flowed on the left. Snow-capped Mount Hood stood behind them.

Even Erin was impressed. "This is the most beautiful spot I've seen since I saw the Grand Tetons in Wyoming. Shane, someday I hope to take you to visit our home there—rolling plains, towering mountains, and all the hunting and fishing your little Oregon heart could stand."

Shane noticed a 1962 red and black Cadillac convertible on the side of the road. The car looked

abandoned. Nobody was even near the vehicle. Marty noticed it too. He yelled as they slowly passed by, "Anybody there?"

Kosy cupped her hands over her mouth, "Nobody but us chickens."

"Okay, enough from the peanut section," Marty pulled on her hair. He pleaded with Shane, "Let's put up the top. It's quite a bit cooler here along the river."

Shane flashed his lights at Bowie. They both pulled over just ahead of a man who was walking along the road. Shane started to put the top up, addressing the oncoming stranger. "Is that your brand new Caddie back there?"

"Sure is, Sonny," the man answered. "I ran out of gas. An $8,000 car that won't run without twenty-five cents' worth of petrol. Incredible, isn't it?"

"Why does everyone call me 'Sonny'?" Shane thought to himself. "Well, you can't leave that new car alone on this road. I have a full gas container I can give you. It

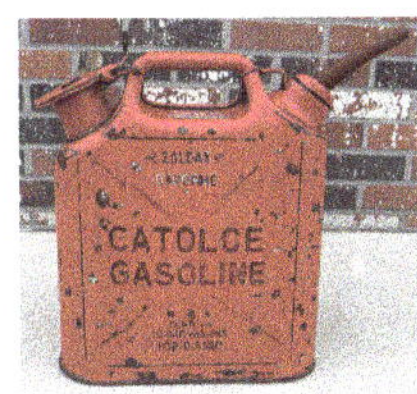

has my name on it, but you can keep it. Just pass it along to someone else who needs it. Also, take this tract and read it, passing it along with the gas can. Is it a deal?"

"Sure, kid." The man was relieved, "It's a deal. I couldn't pay you anyway. All I happen to have is a Standard Oil credit card. You really saved my day. I have a critical engagement back in Portland with a minor league baseball player. Thanks a lot."

Shane handed the man the can and a 'God's Simple Plan of Salvation' tract with Grandpa's address on it. "Now remember the deal. Pass this along with the can, after you read it, of course."

The thankful pedestrian handed Shane one of his business cards. "If you're ever in San Francisco, look me up. Really, I mean it. You've saved me from missing a crucial meeting. I won't forget it."

As Shane finished putting the top up, Erin read the man's business card. "Mr. Carson Dundee—New Personnel Director of the San Francisco Giants."

"Wow, he works for the Giants. He must know Willie Mays personally. Hey, Mr. Dundee," Shane yelled, "thanks for the card. I'll see you in San Francisco someday. And tell Willie Mays I'll watch him in the World Series this fall." Mr. Dundee waved.

As they passed the Bonneville Dam, Bowie pulled into a gas station. "I need to check the horses. This'll be our last stop until we get to Pendleton. If you want a root beer or something, it's now or never."

Shane let Marty drive the rest of the way. On both sides of the river, there were golden waves of wheat.

Monstrous harvesters were already separating the grain from the stalks. Other fields were still irrigated by long aluminum pipes ending at huge wheels that continually circled the fields, leaving large balls of green and, later, golden wheat. This new automated method eliminated the tiresome task of manually moving the pipe every four hours.

The afternoon sun made it seem as if the blue sky would meet the golden fields forever. Erin was again impressed. "There are some awesome color combinations here, Shane."

The tired teens pulled into Pendleton at dusk. The milk cows were just being herded into the barns. Bowie directed them to the Sweet P Ranch just north of the city. Everyone crawled out, hoping to hit the shower.

Bowie introduced his relatives, "Listen, gang, this is my Uncle Two Tall Pinetree and his family. That cutie over there is Princess Ann Pinetree. She just won the title of Miss Teenage Nez Perce of Umatilla County. Ain't she pretty?"

Ana Pinetree blushed, but you couldn't see the color; she already had a lovely dark complexion. Bowie had not exaggerated; she was beautiful. Her olive skin made her straight hair look as black as midnight.

"Well, I'm sure this crowd is tired, hungry, and in need

of some cleaning up," Mrs. Pinetree tried to rescue Ana. "Girls follow me, boys to the left." No one moved yet. They all were still gawking at the beautiful Native American princess.

Marty caught Shane's attention. "Hey, that Princess Ana is really a knockout, isn't she?"

Now it was Erin coming to Shane's rescue, "Shane really didn't notice, did you?" He received an incentive elbow nudge in the rib cage. She hoped he'd get the hint, so she wouldn't have to kick him in the shins, which was more painful.

"Well, Marty, it's kind of hard not to notice," he defended himself. "But, I'll leave that enjoyable decision up to you." Shane rubbed his ribs and smiled at Erin.

Kosy addressed Mr. Pinetree, "Is it always this hot over here?"

"I suppose you already know the Cascade Range keeps most of Oregon's moisture on the west side. The clouds are usually dry by the time the hot winds have pushed them over the mountains to us. We have cold winters and hot summers. Did you notice a change in the landscape after you left The Dalles?"

"Yeah, we did," Marty concurred. "It changed from evergreen to mesquite and brush. The difference was very dramatic. The temperature change was also amazing. We stopped to take the convertible top down. How hot does it get around here?"

"Pendleton has the dubious honor of holding the record for Oregon's hottest day in recorded history—119 degrees," Mr. Pinetree informed them, "but don't worry yourselves into an unnecessary sweat. That was 64 years ago, in 1898."

The ranch house bespoke of Native American heritage. These people were obviously proud of their Nez Perce roots. A thick wooden bench with carved horses as a backrest looked inviting. Shane noticed the unusual furniture. "Is this whole Pinetree family steeped in horse tradition?"

Princess Ana Pinetree was already attracted to Shane. "The Nez Perce were always great horsemen and excellent horse breeders. It was our people who developed the Appaloosa; we even sold many horses to the Army. Unfortunately, the U.S. troops were mounted on some of our own fine horses when they caught Chief Joseph just forty miles short of the Canadian border. He lived and died just sixty miles from here. His grave site is visited often in Wallowa."

Marty tried to catch Ana's attention. "Do people go there to worship him? Are you related to him?"

"Yes and yes," Ana answered Marty, but still kept looking directly at Shane. "Many of our people are spirit and ancestor worshipers. Since Bowie's dad and my dad are brothers, I, too, am a great-great-grandchild of Chief Joseph."

Mr. Pinetree had just come back from putting the horses in the barn. "Enough of our history tonight. You cowboys and Indians will want to clean up and eat. We have an old Indian specialty tonight—tacos and burritos!"

Native American artifacts decorated every part of the living room. A detailed and colorful woven blanket hung opposite a beautifully framed picture of Chief Joseph. But it was the huge mounted buffalo head that really caught their eyes.

The supper had a south-of-the-border twang to it, but the dessert was Alaskan Delight. Shane, Marty, and Bowie shared the same room. Two of them got the bunk bed, and the coin-toss loser slept on the floor cushion.

Marty made sure he won by using his two-headed quarter. Shane was wondering why Marty always won the toss. There was something fishy about that coin, and he promised himself he'd examine it before the next toss.

It was Snoresville until about five in the morning. Three sleeping teens were rudely awakened by Mr. Pinetree beating on the door and yelling into their room, "Get up, boys! THE BARN'S ON FIRE!"

9 - The First Rodeo

Three boys jumped out of bed, quickly pulling on their jeans. When they reached the porch, they saw the barn was completely engulfed in flames. No one could get close to the fire.

"Get your pickup and car away from the barn," Mr. Pinetree yelled. "Put 'em over on the other side of the house. We can't save the barn, nor the animals in it. What we need to do is soak down the house. Hook up the hoses."

The girls stood wrapped in colorful blankets, watching from the porch. When Two Tall Pinetree gave orders, the boys grabbed the garden hoses and hooked them up to the outside faucets.

Kosy had tears in her eyes as she listened to the painful sounds of animals trapped in the fire. She always felt deeply for those suffering. "Bowie lost his rodeo horses. How awful!"

As Bowie and Shane soaked down the west side of the house, they heard fire engines approaching. It was already too late to save any of the barn. The firefighters extinguished the blaze and took over watering the house.

Shane tried to console Bowie, "I'm really sorry, Buddy. I guess this means you're out of the calf roping event, as well as losing two fine horses." Marty added his condolences.

The heavyweight Native American reacted with fury. He stomped around the yard, letting out loud yells. No one present wanted to cross Bowie. When he finally settled down, his voice rang out, making the leaves on the trees shake, "I'LL GET THOSE OUTHOUSES IF IT'S THE LAST THING I DO."

Two Tall Pinetree was trying to calm his nephew down. "It's not as bad as it looks, Bowie."

"What do you mean, 'not bad'?" Shane was shocked by Two Tall's calmness. "Bowie loses two horses, you lose your barn and all your animals, and you say, 'That's not too bad'? Did I hear that right?"

"Well, the loss of the barn and animals is regrettable.

We thought we had everything under control," Two Tall answered with his square jaw set firm. "I never thought they would stoop to this low level. This is really scary. They've gone way too far for a measly rodeo trophy."

Marty was becoming too curious to keep silent any longer. "Who are THEY? WHAT'S going on around here? Would someone who knows more than I do, kindly fill us in?"

"Well, we might as well fill you in," Two Tall started. "We had some premonitions of foul play. I'd received a few anonymous phone calls demanding that Bowie stay in Lebanon until after the rodeo."

"You've got to be kidding." Shane questioned Mr. Pinetree's statement. "Is this rodeo stuff really that serious?"

"You wouldn't think so," Two Tall said, wrinkling his forehead. "I don't think so either. But Bowie is a natural. If he wins first place in two events and places in two others, he could win the *All-Around Cowboy* buckle. Apparently, someone really doesn't want that to happen."

"That's really cute," Erin said, "that a Native American can win the *All Around Cowboy* buckle?"

Bowie smiled, changing his previous scowl. "It's funny. I think that's exactly why someone doesn't want me to win it."

Shane was shaking his head in disbelief. "Really, Bowie, this is 1962, not 1862. Are there still people who are prejudiced against Native Americans? I thought they all faded away with the buckboards and covered wagons."

Bowie reminded Shane, "You lived around Mexicans in California. Were there any prejudices against them in your area?"

"Yes, I did notice it."

"And what do you think old Engelbert Farnsworth III is doing when he calls me names? I know he's mean and ornery with everyone, but he treats me worse than a skunk."

"What are you going to do now, Bowie?" Erin asked, her eyes moist with concern for her friend.

Bowie stayed confident. "I came up last weekend and left my real rodeo horses at my cousin's farm across town. The horses lost in the fire were just two unfortunate steeds, not my good rodeo horses."

"Then you were anticipating trouble," Shane noted. "Why didn't you include us in on the secret?"

"There was a chance, a slim one, that we wouldn't see any trouble. I didn't want to worry you unnecessarily."

Marty was ready to preach, but he decided to tone it down a bit. "Bowie, that's what friends are for. You didn't even give us a chance to turn this situation over to God."

"But really, guys, we weren't expecting anything this severe," Bowie explained. "We thought, at worst, they would try to steal the horses. We were even willing to let them do that, so they'd think they'd beaten me. My uncle even tied up his watchdogs to make it easier for them."

Two Tall Pinetree put his hand on his forehead and grimaced. "We had no idea they'd go this far."

"How do you know THEY started the fire?" Erin questioned. "Could it have been an accident?"

"It would be almost impossible for this to happen by accident TONIGHT," Two Tall said. "Usually, fires burn from the inside out, not the outside in. The firemen will likely prove it was arson."

Mrs. Pinetree consoled her husband, "We do have insurance; that's helpful. We took turns watching the barn all night. It was my turn to watch. I had my  eyes on it all the time. I saw nothing until the whole barn was instantly engulfed in flames. Now it is just a pile of smoldering ashes."

"We'll survive," Two Tall promised. "Let's get some grub and hightail it over to the rodeo grounds to cheer Bowie on to victory."

"One more comment," Shane insisted. "It seems to

me the most likely person or persons responsible for this crime would be associated with the kid Bowie has to beat, right?"

"It could be," Two Tall retorted, "or a group of people not wanting to see a Native American win All Around Cowboy. We have some ideas, but no way to prove anything. Let's keep our eyes peeled for anything suspicious at the rodeo. We want Bowie to have every fair chance to win that trophy."

Bowie had entered four events: calf roping, bull riding, saddle bronc riding, and bareback riding. Calf roping was the only event in which he rode his own horse. His cousin had them ready at the arena.

Each rodeo event was grouped by age and experience. Bowie competed in the teen group for experienced riders. The weather was perfect—hot and dusty—great for sunbathers and soda vendors. The rodeo had a lively atmosphere, full of good horses, fierce bulls, scared calves, fancy-dressed girls, rugged cowboys, and barbecue.

Bowie's first event was BAREBACK RIDING. Obviously, there is no saddle, nor reins to control the horse. The rider has to stay aboard for eight seconds if he expects to win anything. The horse jumps, plunges, and bucks while the rider puts the spurs to it.

The announcer yelled, "From

Lebanon, Oregon—Bowie Pinetree. RIDE'M COWBOY!"

"For Bowie, let's call it RIDE'M INDIAN," Travis Pinetree said, correcting the announcer. Bowie's parents joined the cheering fans. Ana Pinetree quickly shared the morning's events with them.

The glee club from Lacomb went wild when Bowie broke the gate. "RIDE'M BOWIE. HANG ON, INDIAN."

Six seconds, "STAY ABOARD, BOWIE," Shane yelled over the girls' heads. Seven seconds, then eight. The buzzer blew, and Bowie flew. He hit the ground standing up and running hard for the fence.

"All right," Shane yelled as he spilled his popcorn in Erin's hair. "Sorry, kid, guess I got a bit excited."

Bowie had an hour break before his next event. Marty pushed a paper plate towards him. "Would you like some western-style barbecue ribs?"

"Not now, thanks," Bowie replied politely. "The only ribs I'll have are under me. My next event is bull riding, and I can't do that on a full stomach." As everyone heard Bowie's stomach rumble, they smiled at his hungry joke.

Kosy, standing closest, teased, "Wow, Bowie, your stomach sounds like you haven't eaten in days." Bowie smiled and gave her a thumbs up, patting his stomach in agreement.

BULL RIDING: In this event, the competitor—cowboy or Native American—holds onto a long rope looped around the bull. Spurring isn't required; the goal is to stay on for eight seconds. Bowie explained, "This event is dangerous because of the bull's temperament, and every bull knows how to use its horns."

The peanut gallery took their cheering positions. Bowie hit the arena, one arm waving and his hat flying. Being thrown up in the air and slammed down on a sharp backbone was not for cream puffs.

Bowie hung on, but not for eight seconds. After just seven seconds, he was thrown up in the air, and as gravity would have it, brought suddenly back down to earth. The thud shot through Kosy and Erin.

The bull was not one bit amused. The one-ton fury turned on its hind legs. With a head-and-horn-first charge, he tore after Bowie, dust flying and girls screaming. Kosy was the loudest. "RUN, BOWIE, RUN." This excitement gave Kosy a chance to trim her fingernails with her teeth.

"PUMP THOSE LEGS, SON," Bowie's mom yelled above the rest.

Bowie was still dizzy from hitting his head on the ground. He wasn't as alert to the bull as he usually was, or as he should have been. Before

he could react, someone pushed him from behind and into a barrel. The rodeo clowns rolled him away from the 2,000-pound, angry bull, which seemed intent on forcing a cowboy trophy onto its horns.

"That was too close for comfort," Erin sputtered with a shudder. As the clowns diverted the bull to the side of the arena, Bowie jumped safely behind the protection panel.

SADDLE BRONC RIDING would be an afternoon event. The Bowie fan club went for a break, encountering him at the back of the rustic, wooden bleachers. Bowie was dusting himself off. "I'm still in the running for first place. If I can ride that bronc for a full eight seconds, it'll all come down to my time in the calf roping."

Shane still had his idea on the burner. "Who's close to you, you know, tied for first place?"

Bowie scowled. "A dude named John Outhouse, if you could believe that! He's a jerk with a capital 'G,' if you know what I mean."

"That's spelled with a capital 'J,' Bowie," Erin, who always earned an 'A' in her English classes, felt compelled to correct him.

"I know how to spell it," Bowie reminded her, smiling through the dust on his face. "When they're a definite triple zero, like John Outhouse, I spell it with a capital

'G.' Get it? I also spell it that way to see if anyone's actually paying attention. And thank you, Erin, for noting it."

In the afternoon, Bowie remained close to John. Both of them managed to stay on the bucking broncs for eight seconds, with both receiving the same style score. It would all come down to the calf roping time, just as Bowie had predicted.

Ana Pinetree supported her cousin, Bowie. "John did a good job, Cousin. You've got to have a good time in the calf roping to beat him and take the silver buckle. John's calf-roping time was 16:35."

Bowie was leading his horse over to the pens. The Nez Perce was coming up soon. Shane patted the horse on the rump. "Are you nervous, Bowie?"

"Do fish swim?" he answered flatly. "Of course, I'm nervous. A lot depends on my horse, Lightning."

Shane cocked his head to the side and made an inquisitive face. "Where was Lightning just a few minutes ago?"

"Tied up over there by the rest of the horses."

"Just a premonition I have; an idea. Take off the saddle and blanket, Bowie. I want to check something."

"I only have a few minutes, Shane."

"If I am right and you don't take off the saddle, you'll have another saddle bronc ride instead of a calf roping event.”

“Okay, Little Buddy, but help me.” Bowie started ripping off the stomach straps.

When they removed the saddle, Shane turned the blanket over, and discovered a large cockle burr. “Just as I thought. The old burr-under-the-saddle routine. This is a trick as old as Billy the Kid.”

Bowie looked around to see if anyone else was as interested in this discovery as they were. He clenched one fist and slammed it into his open palm. “Wow!,” he thought, as he stared in awe at a highly customized motorcycle belonging to one of the Outhouse gang. It was a mighty bike with a unique design, but it wouldn’t win any trophies at this cowboy event!

“Why, those bums. I could’ve gotten hurt. They don’t care for anyone or anything except winning that stupid trophy and buckle. I’m going to frost their hide with a good time.”

Shane rejoined the Lebanon glee club with a burr in the palm of his hand. “Those nasty guys are going to pay for this someday,” Marty promised.

Erin pushed Marty’s head down so she could see. “Pay attention now. Bowie is coming out.”

Princess Ana Pinetree was screaming as she moved closer to Shane, “Come on, Bowie, give it your best. SHOW THEM BUMS.”

This one-of-a-kind customized motorcycle belonged to the Outhouse clan. Bowie wondered whether this experimental design was comfortable and safe.

10 - Native American Family

Bowie's final rodeo event was calf roping. He entered the arena, swinging his rope. The calf jumped around nervously, with Lightning staying close by. Bowie knew his first throw had to be perfect; there was no time for mistakes.

Bowie's loop landed perfectly. He moved so quickly newcomers struggled to see what happened. The Nez Perce teen jumped off Lightning as the horse stopped, threw the calf, tied three legs, and finished with speed.

Bowie finished in 15.47 seconds. Part of the crowd cheered wildly. Popcorn flew, friends hugged, and Ana gave Shane a more extended hug than the others. Erin noticed and felt a pang of jealousy.

When the hoopla and congratulating had settled down to a small roar, Erin grabbed Kosy and headed for the powder room to check out their hairdos and such. That's when Ana made her move. She quickly scooted over as close as she could to Shane. There was hardly a hair's breadth between them.

Ana wanted to make friends with Shane as fast as possible, maybe even before Erin got back. "Are you actually interested in participating in the rodeo?"

"Not really," Shane didn't want to hurt Ana's feelings. "When I hit the ground, I want it to be on my feet, not on my back, and certainly not on the horns of a red-eyed, sharp-horned, charging Brahma bull. I'd rather sit here in the stands and have thrills running up and down my back instead of a mad-as-a-hornet horse."

"What do you think of our rodeo? Have you ever been to such a gala event?" She was really pouring it on; she had so little time left.

"This certainly is the place to be if you like action or are wearing cowboy boots. I noticed these guys sure

walk funny, though. Most of them look like they were still in diapers when they broke their first horse. I was thinking if Shakespeare ever attended one of these events, he would probably say, 'Behold, what manner of men are these who wear their legs in parentheses,' or something like that."

Ana, lively and determined, wanted to impress Shane. She showed him a photo of poaching victims. Shane didn't find it funny—he disliked poaching—but Ana used it as an excuse to laugh anyway.

With that excuse, the young, beautiful Native American

Princess laughed so hard she fell on Shane's lap. He had to grab hold to prevent her from falling off the bleachers.

Murphy's Law would have it that Erin should now reappear, which she did. She and Kosy noticed the good-time kids were literally falling all over each other. Erin's eyes turned from blue to green. "If Ana Pinetree doesn't watch it, they'll have to change her name to Lame Deer, or Limping Doe." She quickly returned to her place between Shane and the lovely princess.

Bowie received his first-place trophies for two events and the coveted silver buckle for All-Around Cowboy. The money he received was enough to pay for the horses he lost, as well as Shane's costs for coming over with him.

"Winning is fun, isn't it, Bowie?" Kosy gleamed, showing she was proud to be the friend of this Native American who had ground-in dust and dirt all over his big frame. She held up his trophies and buckle for everyone to see.

"Yeah, it looks like it's all over for John Outhouse. "Maybe someday we'll catch those guys at their own game," Travis Pinetree hoped.

There was much to do before the kids headed back to

Lebanon. They still wanted to visit Bowie's friends and relatives on the reservation. Shane wanted to learn more about Nez Perce customs and culture.

They felt it necessary to report their suspicions about the Outhouse gang to the local authorities, especially Officer Elk Looks Back, one of Bowie's uncles. Shane was impressed with this well-dressed Nez Perce.

Elk Looks Back was right on it, "This is more serious than I thought. I'll make a detailed investigation and thorough scanning of the barn area. If I come up with anything concrete, I'll get in touch with you."

Bowie drove them to the Umatilla Indian Reservation. He explained, "Some of my friends and relatives live here." They stopped at a rundown trailer with a rusty pickup out front and old car parts in the yard. Only a little grass grew, and a huge German Shepherd greeted them, wagging its tail.

Erin was leery about getting out of the car. "The dog!" She exclaimed. "I've had numerous bad experiences with dogs that were never supposed to bite. They always said their bark was worse than their bite. I found out the hard way their bite was worse than I thought."

"It's all right, Paleface Princess. Dogs smile by waving their tail." Bowie eased her fears. "Besides, Old Fireyes has chased too many sticks. He has nothing but nubs for teeth. He might try to lick you to death, though."

Bowie felt a little awkward about the disorder. "Not all my relatives are as neat as the Two Tall Pinetrees. But I'm sure you'll like Uncle Running Deer Sagebrush. He's a really nice guy once you get to know him."

Kosy followed Bowie to the front door, stepping over a broken manifold and three rusted-out pistons, noticing  a pile of old tires next to the wall of a storage building close to the trailer. "Is he really your uncle?"

"Not exactly, Kosy, but it's easier to call him Uncle Running Deer. Just calling him Running Deer feels too familiar and doesn't show proper respect for elders. Mr. Sagebrush would be too formal. So, we call all our adult relatives 'Aunt' and 'Uncle'—it makes it feel closer. Do you like that idea, Kosy?"

Once inside the house, the white kids felt more comfortable. It was a typical American-style home, a bit cluttered, but homey. A humongous mountain of a man greeted them in the hallway and motioned for them to enter the living room. He even towered over Bowie. His shirtless belly had so many stress marks, it looked like a Linn County hunter's map.

Mr. Sagebrush excused himself, then returned quickly, wearing a soft leather deer-hide shirt. Shane wondered how many deer hides were used to make a covering that big!

After initial introductions, they were invited to sit down and share some Pepsi and deer jerky. Crying Breeze Sagebrush was making popcorn. Unintentionly, Shane opened up a touchy subject. "How much land do you own, Mr. Sagebrush?"

"That is an interesting subject, Paleface. We Nez Perce never thought land belonged to anyone." He began waving his hands in the air. "The land belonged to all of us. A warrior could own a horse, a tepee, and hunting equipment. His family might even own hides or household items, but the land was always community property."

Shane backed off a bit. "I hope I didn't say something to offend you, Mr. Sagebrush."

"You're a good kid, Shane," he countered. "Call me Uncle Running Dear, please. No, you didn't offend me. I just thought you might be interested in what we believed, and still believe, although we can't practice what we believe."

Marty motioned for him to keep talking. "We're all ears."

"Well, if I can take that literally, I'll call you guys the Elephant Gang!" Running Deer Sagebrush slapped his knee and bellowed like a bull. It was evident he was self-entertained. The rest just smiled. Erin covered her ears with her hair.

"In the old days," the big Native American continued, "the land was jointly held. No one individual could claim it or exploit it. No tribe had the right to sell it, especially not to strangers, and certainly never to the white man. As the Native American saw it, one could not sell the land any more than he could sell the air or sea. For many good reasons, we called the land 'Earth

Mother.' As long as we were controlled by the sun, rain, wind, and snow, we felt we could not control the earth. Have you ever been at the mercy of a blizzard?"

Erin nodded affirmatively. "We certainly have, out in cold Montana, many times. It's very frightening. You can't see your hand in front of your face, and you need a rope from the house to the barn to make sure you can get back and forth without getting lost. I'd like to ask you a personal question, Mr. Sagebrush. I mean Uncle Running Deer. If you were to die today, do you know where you would spend eternity?"

"That, my White Friend, is a big question I don't even have a small answer for. I'm not sure. I've heard what the white man says about God's Son, Jesus Christ. That's certainly an interesting story. I've always accepted the beliefs I was raised with since my childhood. I see no reason to change now."

Shane thought it was time to hit the trail. "We have a tract you might consider reading. It could help you

understand more. We really appreciated the snack. Bowie has one more stop he wants us to make before we start our six-hour drive home."

Bowie directed them to a modern ranch-style house on a hillside. "This'll be a contrast from our last stop. Mr. Greentree is the Nez Perce councilman in this area. It's an elected position. He also teaches Native American History at Eastern Oregon University in LaGrange."

Bowie wasn't wrong. A well-kept and newly-cut lawn greeted them as they parked behind a yellow, 1962 Chevy pickup. Mrs. Greentree met them at the door with three small Greentree children hugging her legs.

Leaning Fawn Greentree patted the tykes on their heads. "We call them Greenshrubs when they're this small. Congratulations, Bowie. I saw the whole rodeo on TV. You deserve every accolade they gave you."

Bowie was embarrassed again, although you couldn't tell it because of his skin color. "Thank you, Auntie, these are my good friends from Lebanon, er ... Lacomb, I mean."

More soda pop and sandwiches met them when they entered the well-equipped kitchen. Beef jerky seemed to be regular fare at all the Native American homes. They had just walked over a thick, plush carpet and noticed many Native American artifacts on the walls representing three hundred years of Nez Perce history. As Bowie said, this was a definite contrast to the last home they had visited.

Erin liked this place better; at least she didn't have to watch where she stepped with her cowgirl boots. "What a lovely home!"

Mrs. Greentree smiled. She liked to be complimented; most people do. "Would you two girls like to see the rest of the house?"

"We sure would," was heard in unison.

Leaning Fawn escorted them down the hall. "The room

on the right is ..."

Mr. Greentree was interested in Shane's attempts to catch the poachers. "The day has long passed since three buffalo robes were traded for one white man's blanket. Poaching is profitable. We also have Tribe members poaching here on our reservation. We have regulated seasons, too. But we don't need to purchase a license or tags. I detest poaching. Its effects are long-range and very disastrous. Have you considered setting a trap for them?"

Marty perked up his ears. "What do you mean by TRAP? What do you have in mind?"

"Well, poachers are not extremely intelligent people. Get a mounted deer head and skin. Set it up in the woods by a place where they're liable to pass. Take a camera, and film them when they're shooting."

"Great idea," Shane complimented Mr. Greentree. "We'll try it when we get back. Marty, your Dad has a few mounted heads, doesn't he?"

Bowie headed for the phone. "I'm going to check in with Officer Elk Looks Back before we leave." He dialed the police station. "Sure, I'll tell them, stand by. He said he found four steel hunting arrow tips in the ashes, along with a few busted balloons in the woods. The balloons smelled like gasoline. He wants to know what we make of it."

Mr. Greentree reasoned, "I think the balloons could have been filled with gas and thrown from the woods without anyone noticing them."

"And they could have lit an arrow, shooting the back side of the barn from the edge of the woods," Shane

added. "No one would see anything until the whole outside of the barn burst into flames, which is exactly what Mrs. Pinetree said had happened."

Bowie agreed, "That's the same conclusion the officer had. No tracks of man, beast, or vehicle were found around the barn, although there was plenty of disturbance in the woods."

"Just a small suggestion for the officer," Mr. Greentree finished. "Have him check all of John Outhouse's friends or relatives who might be members of the archery club or have purchased any of that kind of equipment lately. I'm sure the insurance company will want to find the guilty party."

11 - Setting a Trap

Monday was going to be a big day. Classes would start at Lebanon Union High School. Shane had never been to a large school of 1500 students. He was going to be a little fish in a big pond, but that didn't bother him too much. He was looking forward to the challenge, especially the wrestling season.

When Shane got home from Pendleton, he found a message waiting for him from the Sleens, the other family who shared the log bridge with the Woods. The next day, when he knocked on Mr. Sleen's door, an old friend greeted him warmly.

"Come in, Shane. Do come in. It's good to see you again. I hope you and Kosy stay around for a long time. Remember when you used to peel chittem bark off the trees on the backside of our property and sell it for $3 a sack after you dried it."

"I sure do, Mr. Sleen. What can I do for you now?"

Mr. Sleen motioned for Shane to sit down on the porch swing. Beverly Sleen handed him a glass of iced tea with a slice of lemon. "I understand you helped catch one of the poachers by purchasing his car. You even had Sergeant Kochian right there for the arrest.”

Shane sipped his tea and then nodded his head.

“Well,” the angry farmer continued, “I lost one Jersey cow last month to the poachers’ spotlight. Surely, with a beam that bright, they could tell the difference between a slow, domesticated cow and a swift, wild deer. Anyway, they shot my favorite cow. I didn’t want to risk it again. I bought some cans of white paint and sprayed ‘C O W’ on all twenty of my remaining Jerseys!”

Shane felt sorry for his long-time friend, “Didn’t that resolve the problem for you, Mr. Sleen?”

The milk farmer was getting madder by the minute. “After I buried my favorite cow, I thought it would. Come out here, and look at my prize bull that won first place at the Linn County Fair.”

Shane followed Mr. Sleen outside. Dennis, using a flashlight, directed Shane to where a dead bull lay on its side. Mr. Sleen aimed the beam at its midsection. In the center of the painted 'O' was a large hole. "NOW THOSE BUMS ARE USING MY HERD FOR TARGET PRACTICE!" he shouted, his fists clenched in anger.

The farmer jerked erect and his thin face flushed, "I explained all this to Sergeant Kochian. He can't come out here and protect my herd every night. What am I going to do? Do you have any plans or suggestions?"

Shane wanted to help his friend and stop the poaching. "I have a plan to catch them. I'll need this hide. In the dark, from a distance, it could look like that of a white-tailed deer. Also, do you have a camera with a telescopic lens?"

"Come back in a few hours, and the hide will be ready. You can use my camera. In fact, you can keep it if you're able to stop these hoodlums."

Marty and Shane spent all morning setting up the trap along Roaring River Road. Mr. Lynch contributed an eight-point mounted deer head. The hide was draped over a barrel and partly hidden in the bushes, making the decoy very convincing.

"Now we have to wait. That's always the hardest part," Marty complained a little. "Do you really think they'll come by here?"

"Well, since you don't believe in luck or crossing your fingers, let's pray they do," Shane suggested in a confident voice. "Let's get a few shots of the deer before any action starts."

"Do you have to use the word SHOTS? Won't the word pictures do?" Marty suggested.

Throughout the day, Shane and Marty took turns operating the telescopic camera, making sure its lens didn't reflect the sunlight. They wanted to avoid alerting the poachers again.

Several cars stopped to look at the deer. Since the decoy didn't run when people yelled and threw rocks, the tourists soon lost interest and drove away. The setup must've looked realistic enough.

Lunch time came and went along with a lot of peanut butter and jelly sandwiches, as well as Grandma's chocolate chip cookies. There was even a thermos of cold, fresh, whole milk to wash it down.

"Are we wasting our time or what?" Shane wondered out loud. "If they don't show up before sundown, we'll have to call it quits for today. We won't have enough light to get a good picture."

What had been a bright, burning August sun was now sulking away, planning to hide behind the surrounding mountains. It happened every summer day in Linn County, and each time it was just as beautiful. This particular sunset was not appreciated by two teens who wanted the sun to stand still like it did for Joshua. But it didn't this time.

As twilight signaled the day's end, Shane stroked his chin in thought. "Really, even if we get a picture, that won't prove anything in court," he reasoned. "We'd need to capture the whole event on a 16mm camera for real proof, right, Marty?"

"You can't be serious, Shane. We did all this hard work for nothing! We could have been swimming in The Channels or fishing or even better—wrestling."

Shane had that determined look on his face. He wasn't about to accept a drastic conclusion like that, at least not yet.

Marty was a bit put out. "Well, Murphy's Law is still in effect."

"Yeah, I know," Shane unhappily agreed. "'WHATEVER CAN GO WRONG, WILL GO WRONG.' But God's laws override Murphy's, don't you agree?"

"Right, preacher, but let's hit the road. It's dark enough to use a ..."

"SPOTLIGHT," Shane blurted out softly as a car parked on the shoulder of the road. "Get down, or they'll see us."

"Let's get out of here, or they'll SHOOT us." Marty squeaked as he headed away from the decoy and towards the rear of the batch of trees. Shane followed suit. A bullet hit the stuffed deer head and it went flying.

"We got 'm. Quick, to da bushes and cut off his head. Den we'll drag da rest to da trunk," someone shouted in a voice neither boy wanted to hear at close range.

All three of the poachers started running towards the decoy in the woods. Shane and Marty edged back further into the brush. "Oops," Shane whispered to Marty, "we forgot our lunch bags."

The terrible trio pounced upon the decoy, waving their skinning knives in the air like bayonets. "Hey, Boss, you shot da head clean off," the shortest poacher yelled as he held up the head by the antlers.

"You dummy, can't you see notten? Are you blind, or just stupid?" the boss insulted him. "Dis is a decoy deer. But what for?"

"There are some lunch bags here with a thermos," the third man observed. "What do we do now, Boss?"

"Hightail it outta here, dat's what. I ain't likin dis one bit."

"Should we take a few pot shots into da woods first? We might get lucky and hit someone," the third poacher suggested.

The boss headed for the car. "Sure, knucklehead, with what? Your knife? We left da guns in da car. We'll shoot from da car. Like you said, maybe we'll get lucky and hit something dat's alive."

"Whoa," Shane mused, "we'd better get down and pray at the same time."

Back at their car, the poachers spotted approaching headlights. "No time to shoot into da woods," the boss decided. "Let's get outta here while nobody seen us."

Shane and Marty circled the small clump of trees and hurried to their car. Shane crawled behind the wheel. "We have to follow them and find out where they live."

"Right," Marty agreed, "but we've got to stay far enough behind so they don't get wise. Let them turn around and get across the covered bridge before we begin tailing them."

Shane warmed up the car. "They have only one taillight. We should be able to keep track of them, but since our car is a convertible, it'll be easy to notice. We'll have to maintain a good distance."

The subdued chase began as the poachers crossed the bridge. Marty was using his binoculars to help Shane maintain a safe distance from the poachers. "I wish we could notify the police," Marty remarked, as his twitching leg revealed his nervousness.

Shane kept his focus on their goal. "With the bullet holes in the deer's head and their guns in the car, we might finally have enough to put them in jail."

The good guys followed the bad guys down Snow Peak Road, coming out at Western Plywood Mill. Shane pulled into the log lift and waited for the poachers to turn right or left at the stop sign. "They're turning right," Marty signaled with his hand.

"That means they're going to Albany or Scio," Shane concluded. "We may bring home the bacon yet."

The slow pursuit continued until the poachers turned left at Cottonwoods. Shane marveled, "They sure went the long way around. I don't think they're familiar with all these roads. Maybe they're not from this area. They're headed back to Lebanon now!"

Marty started sputtering. "They're … they're pointing back at us. I … I think they're on to us." The poachers' car lunged forward, bellowing out black smoke and leaving behind five feet of good rubber. Shane followed them, but at a subdued speed.

"They certainly can't outrun us with that old jalopy," Marty blurted out in what he hoped was a confident voice.

"But we really don't know what they have under their hood, do we?" Shane kept them within sight. "If he can lay five feet of rubber in second gear at that speed, he's got more than a standard motor. Did you see all the black smoke pouring out of the tailpipe? I think they're just about to lose their engine."

The pursuit turned into a chase. Shane didn't plan on risking anything to get these poachers. He just wanted to keep them in sight. The '57 Chevy didn't have any trouble keeping up with the souped-up, smoking sedan.

When Shane hit sixty miles per hour, Marty noticed the nose of a police car peeking out from behind a billboard. "Honk your horn, Shane. We need to get the authorities involved in this chase."

Shane began honking and flashing his headlights. The police car tore out from behind the billboard. Marty kept looking behind. "He's got his siren and lights on now."

"Great, because these no-good poachers are as good as in the poky. They obviously don't know this road very well. The next curve can't be taken at sixty miles per hour."

Shane kept up the chase and crept in a little closer. Just at the right time, he pumped his brakes, released, pumped, released, and pumped again until he slowed to forty-five miles per hour.

The poachers were feeling quite confident until they took flight, becoming Lebanon's first Identified Flying Object. Their flight was not as long as the Wright Brothers' at Kitty Hawk, but their landing was noisier. They became a U-shaped ornament on the trunk of a large spruce tree.

Shane pulled over to the corner and jumped out of the car. With his hands raised over his head, he raced to the police car. "Are we glad you crept up behind us! We were chasing three poachers who are now wrapped around Sullivan's tree."

"Okay, Sonny, we'll talk about that later," the officer promised, "right now, I'd better call an ambulance."

Shane turned and ran into Marty, who had followed his lead by running to the squad car. "WHY DOES

EVERYONE ALWAYS CALL ME 'SONNY'? WHY MARTY, WHY?"

"Maybe it's your baby face complexion that makes you look so young," Marty made an observation. "Grow a mustache!"

Shane didn't know whether he liked that conclusion. He was still not quite satisfied. "I can't help it if I was born at a very early age. A mustache, are you kidding? I don't even have peach fuzz yet!"

It took several hours to scrape the car off the tree. An ambulance arrived, taking the poachers to the hospital. Marty was trying to help. "Any rifles found in the car can be traced to prove poaching."

"No need to do that," Officer Freeburg explained. "We found several ducks and a lot of blood in the trunk. I think we have enough to convict these guys, if they ever stand trial. They're really hurting."

Now Marty had time to question Shane. "How's it you knew about this corner and the tree?"

"Well, every time we came back from Albany, Grandpa always slowed down on this curve. It's called Sullivan's Corner. Mr. Sullivan owns that corn field and the big tree. Notice how scarred it is?"

"Yeah, it doesn't even have any trunk

Sullivan's tree that brought the owner a lot of cash!

bark on this side.”

“Good old Mr. Sullivan has insurance on the tree. Whenever anyone hits it, he gets paid.”

“Groooss,” Marty scowled. “Why doesn’t he just cut it down?”

Shane was heading for the car. “I guess he just likes to collect on it from people who drive too fast.”

A lot of excitement rolled through the little Baptist Church on Sunday morning. Several grateful farmers thanked Shane and Marty for following through on the poachers. Pastor Ballentine also added his congratulations. “No reward this time, Shane.”

“Yes, there is, Pastor. Seeing justice done is sometimes considered a reward, isn’t it?”

Monday morning, Shane picked up Marty and Erin. They drove Kosy to Green Mountain Elementary School and then pushed on into Lebanon. He crossed the canal twice to get to 5th Street. There, he spotted Lebanon Union High School, his home for the next four years. He parked next to Bowie, and the foursome headed for the main building.

Shane put his hand out to open the door for Erin. Someone swung it open, placing a dunce cap on his head. "Welcome, scum, to freshman initiation week," crowed Engelbert Farnsworth III. "Shane and Bowie, you two are my slaves for the whole week! WELL, SKIT, SCAT, HOW ABOUT THAT?"

TO BE CONTINUED

Shane Woods Series

Book One: The Snow Peak Robbers
ISBN 978-1-885708-51-9

Book Two: The Strawberry Fair
ISBN 978-1-885708-52-6

Book Three: The Buzzard Butte Poachers
ISBN 978-1-885708-53-3

Book Four: The Eastern Rodeo
ISBN 978-1-885708-54-0

Future books in this 40-book series will depend on reader interest. More book sales may motivate me to publish more of my existing manuscripts.

Author Biography

Dr. Tom Latham

Tom Latham became a Christian while serving in the U.S. Navy, where he began holding Protestant Divine Services whenever his ship was at sea. After  completing his naval service, he spent the next four years at Bible College to further his spiritual journey. He achieved a significant milestone in his studies by earning a Doctor of Ministry (DMin) degree from Luther Rice Seminary.

Tom met Penny Stimpson, and together they began a mission to serve God in Brazil. Their family grew to include three children, six grandchildren, and ten great-grandchildren.

Although Penny was promoted to Glory, Tom continues to serve Christ in Brazil.

To read more details about Dr. Latham's educational journey, visit www.brazilwrestler.com.

Acknowledgments

I want to acknowledge Jesus Christ, my Savior. Without His guidance and grace lifting me from a worldly ditch, this book would not exist. I owe Him more than I can ever repay.

I want to thank my three children, Thomas, Shane, and Kosette, for making life an adventure as we faced the challenges and joys of the mission field in Brazil. Their companionship gave us more experiences than those in my 73 manuscripts, which may soon become published books.

I also want to thank Dave Carlson for his invaluable contribution to the publishing process. His tremendous efforts far exceeded what I could have accomplished alone, and I am deeply grateful.

www.ingramcontent.com/pod-product-compliance
Lightning Source LLC
Chambersburg PA
CBHW050030040726
47599CB00015B/1615